CALL AND RESPONSE

The Challenge of Christian Life

CALL AND RESPONSE

The Challenge of Christian Life

Werner G. Jeanrond

Continuum ● New York

1995

The Continuum Publishing Company
370 Lexington Avenue, New York, NY 10017

© 1995 by Werner G. Jeanrond

Printed in Ireland.

Library of Congress Cataloging-in-Publication Data.

Jeanrond, Werner G., 1955 -
    Call and response : the challenge of Christian life / Werner G.
Jeanrond.
        p. cm.
    Includes bibliographical references and index.
    ISBN 0-8264-0790-0
    1. Christian life. 2. Church renewal. I. Title.
BV4501.2.J385 1995
248.8-dc20

1 3 5 4 2

For
Catherine and Alwin Hartz
in Gratitude

CONTENTS

PREFACE

This book offers some reflections upon the nature and purpose of Christian life in today's world. It does not attempt a comprehensive theological discussion of all aspects of the Christian church. Instead it wishes to contribute to the ongoing discussion on the necessity of church reform. Rather than engaging in a thorough analysis of the reasons for the current crisis of Christian faith and church life, though such an analysis is very important, I wish to explore the spiritual roots and challenges of our individual and communal faith-life today.

I have chosen the title *Call and Response* in order to sum up in three words the essential foundation of Christian faith: God has called us in Jesus Christ to help to build his kingdom. Hence all of Christian existence has to do with understanding this call and with organising our response to this call. I begin by exploring the symbol of the kingdom of God. What do Christians expect of the future? What is the Christian vision of the new life in Christ? How are we to relate to God, each other, God's creative project in this world, and to ourselves? Different ways of how we could respond to God's call in Jesus Christ are assessed. However, in this context the phenomenon of our death as the ultimate challenge to our Christian visions and hopes needs to be discussed. What point is there to respond to God here and now if we have to die anyway? How can the new life in Christ transform our mortal existence already in this world? The Eucharist as the celebration of this new life is the primary place of Christian self-understanding. It combines all

three foundational aspects of Christian faith-life in our
world: proclaiming, celebrating, and sharing the new life.
The criteria of an authentic response to God's call in
Christ developed so far will now inspire the search for
more adequate models of leadership, authority and
church organisation. Finally, I shall explore the mystical
nature of Christian discipleship: How can we today
discover anew God's love for us in our individual and
communal life as Christians?

This book wishes to address every Christian who is
concerned about the present state of crisis in the Christian
churches and who searches for a constructive discussion
of ways of responding better to God's call on all of us to
co-operate with his creative project in this world.
Obviously, coming from a Roman Catholic background
has made me more sensitive both to the rich heritage and
to the particular problems of that one Christian tradition
than to any of the other traditions which I have
encountered and studied so far. However, the point of
this book is not a confessional one. I have tried to present
my thoughts in such a way that every Christian may find
this book stimulating and helpful on her or his journey
towards a more meaningful and richer response to God's
call in Christ on all of us to help to build God's kingdom.
(I refer to God as 'he' in this book, not because I think
that God was male, but in order to avoid the cumbersome
duplication of personal pronouns and thus present a
more readable text.)

The idea for this book arose out of my experiences
during various lecturing engagements with Christian
groups searching for a deeper understanding of the
vocation of individual Christians, of religious

congregations, and of the church as a whole. I am very grateful to all of these groups for sharing with me not only their particular experience of crisis in the church, but also their deeply rooted conviction that our Christian tradition offers rich resources to all those who wish to respond more fully to God's invitation.

I am pleased to acknowledge that an earlier version of sections 1.2–1.4 appeared under the title 'Some Criteria for Church Reform' in *Doctrine and Life* 42 (1992), 354–61; that an earlier version of sections 4.1–4.4 appeared under the title 'The Church: Eucharistic Communion' in *Doctrine and Life* 38 (1988), 530–37; and that in Chapter 5 I have used some of the material previously published as 'Community and Authority: The Nature and Implications of the Authority of Christian Community', in Colin E. Gunton and Daniel W. Hardy, eds., *On Being the Church: Essays on the Christian Community* (Edinburgh: T. & T. Clark, 1989), 81–109. Quotes from the Bible are taken from the *New Revised Standard Version* (New York and Oxford: Oxford University Press, 1989).

I wish to thank the publisher, Michael Gill, for his interest in this book and for his patient encouragement and co-operation during the act of writing. I also wish to express my gratitude to some friends and colleagues for their special support, critical comments and helpful advice. Arne Claesson, Denis Carroll, Cecelia Clegg, Gabriel Daly, Dermot Lane, Adrian Moynes, James Moynes, Rosaleen Moynes, Margaret Spencer, and Carol Stanton have kindly read a draft of this book and offered their comments. Dr Sheila Greene, Dean of the Faculty of Arts (Humanities) of the University of Dublin, Trinity

College, has supported my work on this book with a generous research grant.

This book is dedicated to my friends Catherine and Alwin Hartz in gratitude for their friendship and for their support of my theological work.

WERNER G. JEANROND
Dublin, Pentecost 1994

1

ADVANCING THE KINGDOM OF GOD

What do we expect from the Christian church? What do we expect from God? What do we expect from our future? What vision do we have of the purpose of the Christian church? How do we understand Jesus of Nazareth's proclamation of the nearness of God's kingdom? Do we have a sense of God calling us to contribute to his project with this world?

Before we can begin to tackle these and other related questions we ought to become aware of the situation in which these questions impress themselves on us. Like all generations before us we too experience our time as a time of crisis. What are the particular characteristics of our crisis today?

1.1 Christianity in crisis

There is no shortage of voices which point us to the present state of crisis in the Christian movement. Some claim that we are confronted with a crisis of faith, while others say that we are 'only' witnessing a collapse of faith in the church, though not a collapse of faith in God and Christ. Not that a purely church-related crisis would make things easier to deal with, since it is always through some form of Christian community that we have ourselves been receiving our Christian faith. If now that very community is questioned and even radically challenged, how can we still trust in the message for which it stands?

It is, of course, obvious that today, as always, women and men are searching for authentic answers to their existential quest in just as urgent a manner as people did in past centuries. Moreover, the recent unmasking of many false promises of anti-religious or a-religious models of human organisation, such as communist or totalitarian ideologies or the blind belief in the ordering factor of a progressivist science, has made our search for religious answers even more acute. Yet precisely at this point in history, when one should have expected Christians to fill some of the vacuum created by the collapse of so many anti-human world-views, Christianity, it seems, has lost its nerve and finds itself in deep crisis. Not a crisis imposed on it from outside, but a home-made crisis, a crisis experienced by individual Christians as well as by larger sections of the Christian movement, a crisis of identity, a lack of purpose, a great uncertainty as to how to live a Christian existence under the present conditions of the world, a crisis of the individual Christian and a crisis of the church as a whole.

Christians are engaged in two different strategies of crisis management today: either they constantly apologise for Christianity's ambiguous past, for all the evil committed by Christians in the West, evil associated with attitudes such as colonialism, anti-semitism, eurocentrism, fascism, totalitarianism, exclusivism, patriarchalism, moralism, and dualism; or they hide behind the newly fortified walls of a more or less traditional dogmatism and claim that nothing has changed, that modernity on the one hand and the corresponding process of a Christian *aggiornamento* on the other were tragic mistakes whose effects need to be undone today by retrieving a strong Christian identity which was lost in the course of the emergence of modernity. The claims and actions by the latter group promote further apologies from the former.

Christians, it seems, either regret believing what they do believe or they long for a lost paradise beyond the constant critical and self-critical reflection upon their own identity and its ambiguous tradition.

Inside Christianity too, the signs of crisis are omnipresent. Although members of the various Christian churches may experience the contemporary crisis in somewhat different ways depending on their particular cultural context, many Christians today have become painfully aware of the fact that their beliefs are no longer shared by many of their formerly Christian friends and relatives. Moreover they themselves might find it harder and harder to reconcile their experiences of ancient forms of church organisation or ancient rituals with their ordinary life as mature citizens. In particular, young people, especially in the Western hemisphere, are less and less attracted to join institutionalised forms of Christianity, although they may still maintain a certain sympathy for some radical version of Christian discipleship. However, the institution of Christian community, that is the church, is blamed for its past and present anti-emancipatory stance, for its radical suspicion of anything in our cultures associated with modernity. In Germany, where a formal registration of church membership for tax purposes exists, more than half a million Christians have left the mainline churches in 1992 alone.

Of course, the efforts of coming to terms with modernity undertaken by the so-called liberal wings of Protestantism since Friedrich Schleiermacher (1768–1834) and by a forward-looking section within the Roman Catholic Church both at the Second Vatican Council (1962–5) and also in the course of its preparation, represent brave attempts at changing the general direction of Christianity from an absolutist religion and at opening Christian faith to the many challenges of its newly recognised global context. But as is only too clear today, these efforts to reconsider the role of Christian faith in our global context have only been moderately successful. Large numbers of Christians in different denominations continue to cling to older forms of thinking and behaviour, while at the other end of the spectrum ever increasing numbers of Christians leave the church, though not necessarily their private interest in religion.

Roman Catholic integralists, i.e. those who believe that one accepts either the entire package of Roman doctrines or nothing, are in fact not only defending their view of the Christian faith against the challenges of modernity, but also the particular language and the philosophical as well as authoritarian framework in which that happened to have been expressed many centuries ago. It is true, of course, that for many Roman Catholics the Second Vatican Council proved to be a great shock: too many changes emerged at once for which many believers were not adequately prepared. Similarly, many Catholics who wholeheartedly welcomed the new theological initiatives and religious openings recommended by the Council saw themselves increasingly frustrated by a Vatican bureaucracy which has shown so much disregard for these very initiatives and openings as well as for the conciliar recommendations for change in Catholic attitudes towards the modern world. It is therefore right to argue that '[f]acing modernity, as Catholics had to do during the last quarter century, has meant severe institutional, intellectual, and spiritual stresses and strains'.[1]

Protestants had more time to deal with the shocks of modernity. Moreover, the European culture of the nineteenth century in which Protestantism tried to come to terms with modernity was itself still much more open to the general consideration of Christian matters and attitudes and thus in some respect had its own interest in supporting the transformation of Protestant Christian identity. But this climate of mutual support between some strands of Protestant Christianity and Western culture ended abruptly with the First World War.[2] The experiences of global warfare, the rise of nationalistic states, and the organised extinction of entire peoples in the Holocaust have led to a lasting suspicion within Christianity of any easy alliance between Christian religion and culture.

Still, in spite of its major problems, modernity has remained a challenge to Christian identity. Modernity's promotion of the autonomous subject and its freedom from all kinds of oppression, including the spiritual one, has for many Christians contained an attractive call to search for more emancipatory forms of Christian praxis and thus has led to a continuing debate on what exactly legitimises spiritual and ecclesiastical institution and authority. The rise of feminist groups within the Christian church points most acutely to the need to abandon ancient paradigms of power not only in society, but also in the church. And the various liberation movements emerging from within Christianity itself stress the widely-felt need to develop critical strategies for a transformative social and ecclesial Christian praxis in the modern world.

Moreover, the realm of science and the development of scientific rationality ought not to be ignored by Christians. All our lives are affected by scientific developments.

Christians must reflect on these developments and on their claims to influence our daily existence and our view of the whole cosmos, be it in the field of medicine, mass communication or the computerisation of our life, including the world of children's play. Christians cannot escape modernity; rather it has to be faced, interpreted and assessed critically and self-critically.

However, while the different Christian communities are still occupied with determining their particular approach to the modern world, modernity itself has changed; it is no longer what it used to be. Some philosophers and literary critics would even go so far as to claim that 'modernity' has become an obsolete concept altogether. Instead they propose that we ought to understand our own time more adequately by calling it 'post-modernity'.[3] Strangely enough, some Christian traditionalists have pointed out that the collapse of modernity proves their ancient suspicion against modernity only right. Modernity, as it seems to these anti-modernists, has always been a lost cause. The modern critique of theism, of the church, of the foundations of Christian belief, of Christian social action, and of Christian morality in general has now collapsed. Yet if the anti-modernist propagandists reflected more deeply on the more recent discussion of modernity and its failure, they would not really be so pleased to hear the message of the prophets of post-modernity.

It is true that the propagation of rationalistic knowledge since the Enlightenment has met, for the second time now, with a massive movement of critique. Although the representatives of philosophical and artistic Romanticism in the early nineteenth century had already complained against the surgical, cold effort of grounding all human knowledge on reason alone by pointing to other dimensions of the much richer human experience of the world, they did not doubt the fact that the act of critical reasoning as such was a constituent factor of the human self's approach to reality. Now, however, the second vogue of critique of the Enlightenment model of human thinking, acting and emancipation concentrates on the very foundation of human self-understanding, namely the understanding of the self itself. The self has become the problem, and it appears today that no single theory of the self can promise to reconstruct it once and for all.[4] Rather the human self is seen more as a limit-concept than as a sure foundation of any intellectual understanding or practical action.

This dissolution of the self is not only not experienced by some as a tragic loss of an old friend, but is celebrated by many as a new juncture in human development: away from the potentially terroristic forms of Enlightenment rationality to the endless dance of not-selves. Echoes of Friedrich Nietzsche can be heard here very clearly. More than a century ago he pointed to the failure of any metaphysical operation to provide a sure starting-point for human thinking and acting. It seems that with the advent of post-modernism Nietzsche's insights have borne fruit. God and the self as metaphysical constructs which were able to give meaning to a whole superstructure of human legitimacy have died; or, more precisely, have been unmasked as classic fakes all along. Thus, those representatives of Christian traditionalism who celebrated prematurely the end of modernity may find now that they have not only been freed from an oppressive modern system based on autonomous reason, agency and critique, but equally from the terrors of any *system* of thinking including their own particular one. All systems trying to advance a total claim of one sort or another have been deconstructed by contemporary philosophy. Reason is not dead, but its attempt to ground itself upon an unshakeable foundation has been exposed as impossible.

The post-modern critique of human thought and praxis can also be seen as a potential contribution to the general reassessment of religion. Of course, any systematic claim to exclusive and total knowledge would be rejected by post-modern thinkers. But once all claims to a total grasp of our self-understanding and to a strong ontological certainty are subjected to the post-modern critique, the individual and communal search for experiences of God's presence in our world receives new urgency. Though post-modern thought has a strong dislike of systematic grasps of meaning, it has a surprising likeness to mystical approaches to reality. Like the great Christian mystics, post-modern thinkers are open to rediscover the self beyond the self, reality beyond reality, and God beyond God. Thus, it would be wrong to diagnose a foundational hostility to religion in today's intellectual climate. What is, however, true is that the intellectual climate in the West harbours a fundamental suspicion of any form of dogmatism and institutionalism.

It must therefore not surprise us that with regard to the church today questions are asked such as these: Do we need the kind of church we have now? Is the supposedly essential difference between priests and lay-people a tenable construct? How can lay Christians, i.e. non-priests, contribute more adequately to the life of the church? How can women participate fully in the ministries of the church? How can priests, pastors and ministers be freed for the church and from the stigma of being nothing other than either mere sacramental executives or unskilled social workers? It is often overlooked that the current crisis is not only a crisis of the laity or more specifically of women in the church, but it is equally a crisis of the ordained ministry or its declining numbers. All groups within the church experience that crisis.

On a larger scale one can say that the entire European–North American culture has lost its nerve. A severe self-doubt dominates our discussions of our culture and its development. Its colonial, tyrannic and domineering features are exposed, analysed and rejected. But the commitment to the necessary assessment of the dark sides of both our culture and its Christian underpinning must not be taken to lead to the large-scale abandonment of every aspect of our cultural heritage and its religious dimensions. Surely, to state – and we must state this again and again – that on the whole Christians in the past have often failed to witness adequately to God's good news, is not yet the final verdict on the Christian gospel itself. Rather we must ask anew whether we today can think of ways of being more responsive to God's call in Christ and thus to renew this universe by participating in God's creative project.

Yet while there are many voices which express this Christian self-doubt, there seems to be some shortage of strategies as to how to tackle this crisis. In this book I could, of course, spend valuable time by adding more reports to the existing chorus of disenchanted voices on this crisis and thus invite the reader at least to celebrate the solidarity of the unhappy. But I have decided to follow a different course of action. I would like to invite the reader to reflect with me upon possible ways out of this crisis of the church. Thus, I ask you first of all to acknowledge that there is a crisis and that the escape from it into an illusory world of the past, where all was well and safely ordered, does not constitute a meaningful solution to our current problems with our identity as Christian community. Let us never forget that the past was not all bliss, but has helped to produce precisely this crisis of identity in which we find ourselves today. I would like to encourage all Christians to work together for a better church to which all of us can contribute in our different though equally valuable ways and according to our different God-given talents.

Hence I propose that in the remainder of this chapter we engage in a *constructive* reflection: firstly, on the nature of the church, with special regard to its purpose in God's overall creative project; secondly, on the basis of such a reflection, develop our strategies for a renewed understanding of ministry; and, thirdly, for a reform of the Christian response to God's invitation to help build his kingdom. Thus, before we can tackle the more concrete steps of mapping out how to work together on this Christian project, we must try to renew our basic understanding of this project, and ask once more in what consists the mission of the Christian church in this world.

1.2 The mission of the Christian church in the world

In the many debates on the role of priests, lay-people, women, bishops, popes etc. in the church we often forget the larger context or the overall purpose of the church in this world. Without going here into the depth of a theological text-book we can at least try to reformulate the basic purpose of the church in God's plan as we understand it.

The church is a community of disciples who are

determined to follow Christ in doing the will of God. Thus, the church is primarily characterised by its response to God's call. Its first task must therefore always be to listen again and again to the manifestation of God's will in the history of Israel and in the ministry, death and resurrection of Jesus Christ.

The New Testament employs a number of terms which illustrate the aim of Christian discipleship. John's gospel speaks repeatedly of 'eternal life', whereas the gospels of Mark, Luke and Matthew often refer to the 'kingdom of God' or 'reign of God'. These terms are eschatological terms, which means that they point to a state of divine-human interrelatedness which God wishes to bring about with our co-operation. The proper relationship between God and his creation is not yet achieved. Rather the repeated breakdown of relationships, often referred to as 'sin', characterises our existence. In this situation of broken relationships the community of Christians, the church, is called to help to establish God's kingdom.

For many republican and anti-monarchical people the term 'kingdom of God' may smell foul. Some may find consolation in the insistence by some translators of the Bible that one really ought to translate the Greek basileia tou theou as 'reign of God' and thus avoid the monarchical implications. However, I do not think that the precise choice of translation into English matters here as much as the clarity of what involved in God's promise of an emerging state of harmony between God and his creation. Hence, I propose to continue to use the traditional terminology of God's kingdom but hope to add to the clarification of its meaning.

It is crucial that we see that the church must never be confused with God's kingdom. The church is not the kingdom of God. Rather it proclaims the good news of the arrival of this kingdom and helps to establish it here in this world. The church is therefore not so much concerned with any world to come than with the transformation of this world.

An often-told story may help to expose the tragic misunderstanding of the church's purpose in the world: when the late Irish writer Brendan Behan once came into Parsons' bookshop in Dublin and discovered there a copy of the *Catholic Standard,* he remarked: 'Ah here is the news of the next world.' Is this not the way in which many Christians have thought of the church's purpose, namely to prepare our souls here in this world for the next world? Thus, the true purpose of this world created and loved by God has not always been adequately appreciated. But once we remind ourselves that it is in this world that God's reign is to be established, we cannot afford not to be interested in the state of this globe with all its creative potential and all its present troubles. News of this world, then, is news about the state of God's emerging kingdom.

What precisely is the church to achieve in this world? It preaches God's good news and it develops strategies of acting according to Jesus's liberating message. What is that message? Jesus showed God's closeness to us and he emphasised God's will that we all live in his presence as his free partners, freed from all fear and threatening demons. To accept this God-given freedom takes precedence over all other commitments, be these to one's family, one's temple, one's land, or one's religious law. Jesus's 'relatives' were those who with him did the will of God. His relationship to God was direct and did not need the mediation of a temple cult, though he did not oppose the ministries undertaken by the Levites as long as they served God and not their own status. Jesus proclaimed God's love even to social and ethnic outcasts, such as the Samaritan woman at the well (John 4). God's people are not defined in terms of their citizenship or their sex. And Jesus came to bring back life to the Torah, i.e. the religious law, which was supposed to order the relationships between God and his people, between the people themselves, and between the people and God's creation. The spirit of God determined whether or not certain prescriptions and commands were all right, and not their letter.

We today must make up our mind whether or not we wish to accept this enormous freedom which Jesus proclaimed and whether or not we wish to organise the community of Jesus's disciples according to this new spirit of freedom. In other words, do we wish to accept this spirit as the criterion for judging whether or not we are on the way to co-operate with the coming kingdom of God. If we are not clear about the criteria for discerning the dimensions of God's kingdom, we may be in constant confusion as to where that kingdom is under construction, and as a result we may be misled by all kinds of pseudo-kingdom builders.

One of the most striking features of the kingdom of God which Jesus proclaimed is that *everybody* is invited to become part of it. Every genuine response to God's call is equally welcome and important to God. This is another criterion for judging whether or not we are open to the arrival of the kingdom. Differences in personality, in character and talents are not only not obstacles, but are one of the signs of God's people. However, forms of class-thinking and status-defence are clearly against the will of God.

So far we have identified two features of God's kingdom, namely the freedom from all kinds of oppression, and the radical equality of all of its members. But there is one other feature not yet discussed, and that is the element of surprise. God's presence in our lives does have surprising and at times very unsettling effects.

The Irish writer Patrick Kavanagh expressed this experience of God's surprising presence in a number of his poems.[5] Accordingly God's presence may become suddenly visible to a lonely walker along the canal bank in Dublin, God's presence may manifest itself in women, it may become an overpowering reality in the streets of Dublin or in the fields of Kildare. God's presence is thus neither restricted to official places of organised worship nor can it be managed or controlled by professional religionists or theologians. Rather God's presence happens in people who are prepared to be open and responsive to God. The God of Jesus Christ is and remains a God who surprises us, and his reign will always be greater and more colourful than we imagine and normally allow for. As experienced by the Israelite prophets, by Moses and by Jesus of Nazareth, once one enters into a relationship with Yahweh, one's life begins to change, the dynamics of God's love begins to unfold its creativity. Then God's love overcomes all forms of death: social death, physical death, organised death, accidental death; whatever has been uncreative begins to bear fruit again.

The three criteria established above do not represent an exhaustive list of what we have to take into account when we assess our progress on the way to God's kingdom, but they are nevertheless crucial criteria. Freedom to love, radical equality and the readiness to be carried away by love beyond the boundaries imposed on us by ourselves and by others are signs for the arrival of God's kingdom. Any state of the church at any given time must be measured at least by these criteria. Then questions such as these arise: Are we as a community of Christ's disciples responding to God's call in the way described or are we not? Is our self-understanding as a church marked by a fear of losing our power or by our readiness to embark on a journey with God into the unknown? Do we take our religious institutions more seriously than we ought to? Of course, we do need ways of organising our response to God and of handing on our faith to the next generations. Nobody will seriously question that. But what is put into question in our current crisis is whether or not the spiritual and organisational steps which we have taken are altogether adequate, and whether or not the right set of criteria has been applied for their continuous evaluation. Unless we are prepared to question our self-understanding as a church again and again we may be in danger of using our different forms of ministry too much as self-serving rather than as God-serving.

Let us consider now the nature of ministry in the light of our renewed appreciation of the church's relationship to God's coming kingdom.

1.3 Co-operative ministry

Ministry means first of all 'service'. It is a service to the people of God and at the same time a service to God. One of the greatest dangers of misunderstanding what ministry means in all Christian churches is the concept of

representation. By that I mean that Christians look to
somebody else as the one who is Christian on their
behalf. All too often priests and even theologians are
considered to be a sort of a professional Christian, paid
to be Christian so as to assure that the non-paid Christians
be saved. Such a concept of ministry, though it seems
omnipresent in all Christian churches, is not only wrong,
but diametrically opposed to the arrival of God's
kingdom. God's kingdom can only happen when we all
allow it to happen. God respects our freedom to say 'No'
or 'Not yet' and does not impose his gifts on us. As a
result no priest, pastor or minister can assure the arrival
of God's kingdom on somebody else's behalf. All a
minister can do is to proclaim God's presence in our
midst so that it may unfold its creativity if we listen to it,
accept it and respond to it accordingly. The kingdom is
close when we respond, but remains distant as long as
we do not.

The Second Vatican Council has emphasised anew the
ministerial nature of the entire people of God when it
speaks of the priesthood of all people (*Lumen Gentium*
I,10) and thus joined in general terms the traditional
Protestant understanding of the nature of ministry.
However it then distinguishes between the ministry of the
ordained priests and the ministry of the ordinary faithful.
The ordained ministry is characterised by the 'holy
power' which the priest has and through which he
educates and guides the priestly people. This holy power
of the priest relates to the performance of the eucharistic
sacrifice and the other sacraments. In spite of these
distinctions between ordained priesthood and
unordained priesthood, the text of the Constitution on the
Church (*Lumen Gentium*) points out that these two forms

of ministry cannot be separated. The one makes sense only with the other. That means that the ordained priesthood depends on the people of God, and without the ordained priesthood the people cannot perform the eucharistic ministry.

When one studies the presuppositions of these definitions of priesthood one readily discovers to what an extent the understanding of the ordained ministry in the Roman Catholic Church is linked to the performance of the eucharistic sacrifice. The power to preside over the celebration of the Eucharist is the centre of the Roman Catholic understanding of the ordained ministry. Everything else follows from that. On the one hand that makes good sense since the Eucharist is undoubtedly the best expression of our sacramental understanding of life in God's presence (see Chapter 4). On the other hand the fact is that one cannot isolate the celebration of the Eucharist from our overall effort of responding to God's invitation to build his kingdom. The conflict which may emerge here is the one between the spiritual power which every Christian receives from God in order to respond to God's call according to her or his talents, and the special power which we are told the priest has received to respond to God's will in his particular ministry.

Why is there this 'essential' difference between the ordained ministry and the ordinary ministry? That there is a functional difference nobody will doubt; the fact of the diversity of service in God's kingdom is a welcome feature of this organism as we have seen already. But what about the 'essential' difference? Does it not ultimately favour a two-class system in the church and thus threaten to betray the radical equality in God's kingdom as proclaimed by Jesus? Does it not possibly lead to new forms of alienation instead of overcoming any form of class-difference? Does it not re-introduce a necessity of mediation between God and his people, a mediation so radically challenged and declared unnecessary by Jesus himself?

Once again, the Vatican Council document itself stresses the need for a co-operative ministry, but it does not appreciate enough the problems caused by maintaining an 'essential' distinction between different forms of ministries. However, even if one may wish to question the legitimacy of such an essential distinction, one must take seriously the call in *Lumen Gentium* to all members in the Church to co-operate with each other. Thus, the Vatican Council document's understanding of ministry does not offer anybody an excuse for not looking for better forms of co-operation in Christian ministry. Nor can this document be rightly interpreted as a defence for a clerical class-consciousness, since it puts all the emphasis on the aspect of serving the people of God. Neither clergy nor laity can achieve anything without the other. Hence we all must learn to accept that the kingdom of God can *only* be advanced by working together.

These considerations are important for our reflection on better ways of ministering together, i.e. of serving God and each other in a more co-operative way. They make clear that no amount of Masses said or Eucharists celebrated will accelerate the arrival of the kingdom if the congregation does not at the same time accept their individual and corporate responsibility for this kingdom. No statistics of Mass attendance or indeed any statistics will ever tell us of the speed of the kingdom's arrival. The only means of accelerating the kingdom's arrival is conversion, which means that we review and change our faith practice. And to these changes we must now turn.

1.4 Towards a better church

What do we really expect to happen when we pray in the Lord's Prayer 'Your kingdom come'? Are we only saying these words, though deep down we think that the kingdom would not yet come; or do we really mean what we say? Are we perhaps like the apostle Peter who according to Mark's gospel (chapter 8) did not hesitate to shout 'You are the Christ' when asked about Jesus's identity, but who found it then impossible to accept that such a confession ought to lead to a radical change of lifestyle and expectation. Jesus had to rebuke him and went even as far as calling him 'Satan' for not realising the true meaning and cost of discipleship. A true disciple is not the one who knows everything about Jesus, but the one who follows him by carrying her or his own cross.

Hence when we expect God's kingdom to come in a triumphant way and look forward to view this spectacle from a seat in the front row, we have dramatically misunderstood the nature of this kingdom altogether. Then, like Peter, we need to be reminded that the arrival of God's reign is neither glamorous, nor a spectacle to be viewed from a certain distance. Rather it is a process which can only happen when we ourselves actively participate in it.

It is therefore important for us to understand that looking for a better church means looking for more active ways of working for this kingdom. It means to search for ways in which our particular branch of the Christian movement could help to renew the movement as a whole and thus give it more strength to welcome God's reign. However, in order for any particular church to contribute more vigorously to the Christian movement as a whole, its members would have to contribute more actively to the renewal of their particular community.

Nobody can be a Christian as such; nobody can be a Christian in a social vacuum. To be a Christian means to work with others for God's kingdom in response to God's invitation. However, working in and through a particular network of disciples does not mean one has to become defensive about that particular tradition or setting. In that sense, for example, I am not a Roman Catholic or a Lutheran in order to be a Roman Catholic or a Lutheran, but I am a Roman Catholic or a Lutheran in order to work through that particular tradition for the kingdom of God. The criteria developed in order to assess our co-operation for that kingdom must therefore also be applied here in order to check whether or not my particular Lutheran or Roman Catholic Church tradition does in fact adequately enough promote the arrival of God's kingdom.

We have mentioned some ways already in which we could contribute more actively to the renewal of our particular church tradition. Firstly, as so-called lay-Christians we may wish to stop using the excuse of the poor state of the ordained priesthood for our own inactivity. Instead we could begin to support everybody, priest or lay-person alike, in their vocation to respond to God's invitation to co-operate in his project. Secondly, priests could stop defending their ministry in vicarious or essentialist terms. That means that any form of ministry may now be considered in terms of how it actually promotes God's kingdom rather than what it represents in virtue of its ordination. Thirdly, all members of a parish or congregation could recognise that nobody other than they themselves is responsible for their community's response to God's call. Negatively speaking, one could say that we all have to claim back the church; positively speaking, one could say we all have to become accountable again for our church. The establishment of parish councils and of parish finance committees may be good illustrations for such a first move towards a more co-operative ministry on the parish level. However, such moves are not enough. Even on the diocesan level, on the national level, and on the global level of the church all responsibility must be exercised more co-operatively. The present practice in the Roman Catholic Church, that the bishops rule on all of these levels, has to stop lest people continue to think that this church is ultimately the bishops' or the pope's own business, while laity and priests are admitted to co-operate only at the mercy of the hierarchy.

We have seen already that in the context of the church any form of representation is ambiguous because people may interpret the fact that they have elected a representative as an excuse for their own continuing inactivity. On the other hand the present Roman Catholic system of nominating people from above into committees (such as the Irish commission for the laity) is unambiguously discouraging for any Roman Catholic Christian who would wish to participate more actively and co-operatively with the ordained ministry. Every Christian's honest contribution to the church's mission in this world must be welcome. If it is not, then the church is not on the way to God's kingdom. Therefore, in the absence of any better organisational system, even the Roman Catholic Church would need to develop some form of a synodal system which allows for the participation of every Christian on all levels of our work for God's kingdom.

The present discussion of the admission of women to the ordained ministry in many churches deserves more reflection. Against all understanding of Christian equality, the male and self-elected representatives of some churches are deciding in this matter without any recourse to the church's overall mission as the proclaimer of God's kingdom. One ought to observe very carefully, though, that the necessary campaign for the ordination of women will not lead us into a situation where the theologically questionable concept of 'essentially' different forms of priesthood or ministry is now preserved once and for all by extending it also to women. What I think we need most urgently in this situation is a wholehearted and self-critical review of the entire theology of ministry and ministerial organisation in the church. Some of the criteria for such a review have been discussed in this chapter; others will be added in subsequent chapters.

1.5 Conclusion

Our three criteria for assessing whether or not we are on the way to co-operating with each other for the kingdom of God are: freedom from fear and oppression, equality of service, and openness to God's dynamics of love. But are we really free from structural oppression in the church; do we really experience ourselves as equal, though different, members in the church of Christ; and are we really open for God's, at times anarchical, plots and surprises? Are we not often the slaves of our own traditions, are we not too often focussed on a very unequal distribution of power and responsibility in our respective churches? Are we not afraid deep down that God may want us to change all that?

One of my theology teachers once wrote that the church ought to be much more anarchical against itself and thus more open to God's true *arche*, that means God's true *reign* in our life and world, and even in our church.[6] The essentialist understanding of priesthood and laity may thus be in need of a thorough revision. This revision is not the reason for the crisis in which we find ourselves already. Rather it is one attempt to tackle this crisis from a faithful reflection upon the foundations of God's call on us in Jesus Christ and on our response to this call. Maybe this constructive revision and the current crisis together may produce the right climate in which all of us will wake up to accept afresh our own individual and corporate co-responsibilty for God's kingdom and the call to work together for its speedier arrival.

2

BUILDING THE FAITH COMMUNITY

2.0 Introduction

In the previous chapter we discussed some of the implications of God's call on us in Jesus Christ to help build God's kingdom. We reminded ourselves that the church is not the kingdom, rather the church proclaims the arrival of God's kingdom. And we rediscovered the radical equality of all men and women in God's creative plan for our universe. Therefore any class system in the church, such as the two-class system of priests and laity, has to be rejected. We also saw the need to think about new and more adequate structures of our church organisation in response to God's call to all of us to help advance his kingdom. Most of all we realised that our focus on God's kingdom helps us to see all aspects of our concrete Christian existence in a new and possibly different perspective. Thus, we became aware again of the radical urgency of our individual and communal response to God's invitation. We cannot sit back and hope that others on our behalf will be doing the will of God. Rather we ought to recognise that the God of Israel and of Jesus of Nazareth is a creator whose creative project suffers if his creatures are not responding actively to his invitation articulated both in Israelite history and by Jesus Christ and his disciples.

The misunderstanding that only 'official' authorities in the church can legitimately formulate on behalf of all of us what a responsible response to God's invitation consists of, has been most paralysing for many Christians wishing to respond to God's invitation. Thus, the very existence of the church and its leadership has been taken wrongly by many Christians as some sort of a guarantee that by belonging to this church organisation they are already doing the will of God. Hence the ambiguity of our Christian traditions has been overlooked. I say ambiguity because I wish to emphasise that on the one hand it is thanks to our Christian tradition that we know about God's call in Jesus Christ, but on the other hand, it is also partly because of that tradition that we have failed to respond adequately to God's call.

In this chapter we shall attempt to see what we can do, individually and together, in order to respond more adequately to God's invitation to help build his kingdom. Thus, we will have to tackle the difficult problem of the relationship between our individual and communal faith-praxis. Of course, everybody knows that the two are inseparable. But we ought to distinguish more exactly how they are related. Otherwise we run the risk of either confusing the different realms of our faith-praxis or of escaping from one to the other when things get tough.

2.1 Salvation of the individual and creation of the universe

As long as the Christian movement has existed in any formal sense – that means ever since people have begun to respond to Jesus Christ's initiatives – we can observe two trends in the Christian church. One group of people long more for their individual justification or salvation out of this fallen world and into God's intimate presence. Another group of people continue to stress more God's creative project and thus the principal goodness of God's creation in spite of all the experiences of human failure to respond more adequately to this project. This latter group believes in the continuity of God's creative presence, while the first group believes in a radical rupture between the old fallen world and the emerging new world since God's radical intervention in this world through Jesus Christ.

The question whether or not one sides with one or the other of these trends is quite important for one's view of participation in the concerns of this universe. Because if one believes that this universe is basically a fallen one and that the only real way of associating with God means reaching out for a world different from the present one, there is not too much point in participating in communal projects in response to God's call in this present world. In other words, the theory of the radically fallen world tends to encourage individual faith projects, whereas the belief in God's concern for this world tends to promote more of an appreciation of a communal effort, both to protect this world from extinction and to make it better in response to God's call according to which all of us ought to become co-creators of his project. Hence, belief in individual salvation favours individual faith projects, and belief in God's renewal of the invitation to co-create this universe favours more communal answers to God's call.

Before we move on in our discussion of possible responses to God's call we ought to be aware of the possible dangers and distortions in these two trends. The inherent danger in any belief in only individual salvation lies obviously in the implied reductionist view of the universe. God becomes the God of our salvation *from* this universe, the one who calls people away from the mess of this world into a paradise of quite different proportions, from nature to super-nature. Such a model is dualistic, that means it recognises two radically distinct spheres of human existence: the worldly one and the spiritual one, the one where God is absent and the other where God is present. It also stresses the individual side of religion in so far as it promises the individual to be moved eventually fully out of the prison of this world into the presence of God. Communal faith-projects arise here only in terms of the need to remind each other of God's gracious acts of personal salvation. Such a salvation-centred model of Christian faith then concentrates on proclamation and individual conversion, but not on a communal faith-praxis which aims at transforming both our present lives and this world in response to God's call in Christ.

However, a merely creation-centred faith also has its problems. It may be in danger of overemphasising our human activities and initiatives and therefore ultimately of underestimating God's gracious involvement in this world. Traditionally this problem was handled under the rubric 'immanent' or 'transcendent' faith. In modern language one could refer to it in terms of how much do we let God be truly God and human beings fully human without confusing one with the other. Moreover, this creation-project faith may at times ignore the individual needs of people to hear afresh God's liberating and saving word. Thus, it may be in danger of stressing Christian praxis too much to the detriment of Christian receptiveness and proclamation of God's love and grace for every human being.

In my discussion here I shall follow the creation-centred understanding of God's project for this world. But I attempt not to overlook the individual's situation with her or his particular fears and experiences of suffering and oppression, and corresponding longings for personal redemption and salvation.

On the one hand, Israel's experience with Yahweh as expressed in the story of the call of Moses at the burning bush (Exodus 3) reminds us of God's intention to be involved in his people's destiny and to help organise its liberation from oppression through the mediation of faithful people such as Moses. God gave Moses a promise of his divine presence in history. Jesus, on the other hand, invited us to see God as *abba*, that means as a loving parent. While these symbolic expressions do not say everything about God, they offer us important insights into God's care and concern for his people as a whole and for each individual person. We may wish to try and think of God today in even more fitting terms, metaphors and symbolic representations, though we should never speak of God in terms of less than a God who is an involved God and whom we can experience in analogy to a loving and caring parent.[1]

2.2 Christian faith and the political realm: one or two kingdoms?

Every consideration of possible Christian responses to God's invitation to join him in co-creating this world leads the Christian unavoidably into the political arena. If we believe that this world is God's world, we must treat it accordingly. But our Christian concerns will meet with many other publicly voiced projects and concerns for the protection and development of this universe. Do we have as Christians better and more adequate answers in response to political problems, environmental projects, and economic theories? Does our faith in God qualify us better than anybody else for the political tasks in this world? Are we to strive for a monistic, that means one-sided, Christian vision of politics or are we to leave politics to the politicians, economics to the economists, and environmental concerns to the environmentalists and instead concentrate purely on our inner-Christian organisational structures, i.e. the churches and their development and transformation?

This set of questions brings us back to the old Christian theory of the two cities in which we live. In his famous work *The City of God* St Augustine (354–430) wrote that each Christian lives at the same time in two cities, the earthly city and the heavenly city. The earthly city is characterised by our fallen nature and thus calls for ways of containing the evil which we are about to do because of our nature. The heavenly city is characterised by God's gracious presence and represents the ultimate home for our restless souls. In this scheme the world requires political action in order to contain our potential for evil. Politics as such, however, has nothing creative to contribute to God's realm.

Although this is not the place to explore the background and development of Augustine's world-view, it is crucial for us to recognise its impact on later Christian thinking. The Protestant Reformers further developed this theory of the two cities into the theory of the two realms, the worldly realm and the spiritual realm. Martin Luther also took the rotten nature of the world as a sure fact and starting-point in order then to develop his theory of salvation. But this theory was now much more concerned with individual salvation. His question was: How can I find a gracious God? Thus, his primary worry was how God could accept me, the sinner. The answer was found in Paul's Letter to the Romans: 'It is the power of God for salvation to everyone who has faith, to the Jew first and also to the Greek. For in it the righteousness of God is revealed through faith for faith; as it is written, "The one who is righteous will live by faith."' (1:16b–17). Only through faith, Luther concluded, are we justified.

Faith became the magic word of the Reformation against all kinds of misuses of the gospel by the church in Rome. However, it was not always clear what exactly this faith was all about. For instance, also in chapter 1 of Romans one can find important hints towards a more creation-centred faith: 'Ever since the creation of the world his eternal power and divine nature, invisible though they are, have been understood and seen through the things he has made.' (Rom. 1:20).

Luther's question was the medieval question of how we can find forgiveness and grace with God, though now sharpened through the heightened awareness of humanist attention to the individual. To that extent Martin Luther was both a medieval and a modern thinker. But his concentration on personal justification lost sight of God's overall creative project. As a result Luther's theory of politics was confined to state once more that we need political authority to organise us in a way which promises to contain our evil nature, and that God has called for the establishment of both the temporal authority and the spiritual authority. Hence, even political leadership could understand itself to be willed by God, and did not need to be afraid of public unrest from Christian quarters, since Christians must know that God had organised the political authority as well as the spiritual.

It is interesting to note that Luther's concept of political leadership is not that far removed from the Roman

Catholic one of the time. It too considered both pope and emperor appointed by God and therefore legitimately calling for respect and total obedience from all subjects. However, in the Catholic system of the time the relationship between both authorities was less clearly defined. Both existed for the benefit of the people of God, but the power sharing between throne and altar was less clear.

Obviously today we cannot easily accept either system. The radical separation between the two kingdoms cannot be considered adequate in Christian terms since, as I have argued, we as Christians believe in God's concern and care for this world. Thus we have to work for a new relationship between the spiritual dimensions of our faith and our practical involvement in this world.

Unlike in medieval or Reformation times, we today do not exist in a more or less exclusively Christian environment. Rather we live in a radically pluralist context in which not only Christians think and act, but in which many different and often conflicting programmes of government and very diverse forms of general political participation are discussed. We Christians have only begun the learning process of how to come to terms with the two facts that, firstly, our voice is only one among many voices in the global conversation on the nature and future of the world; and also that there is more than one Christian voice to be reckoned with. On the one hand, we have for far too long accepted uncritically the authority structures defended by our medieval predecessors without ever challenging them properly in the light of our understanding of God's creative project. On the other hand, it is well known that those who have attempted critically to rethink these structures have often been censored and excluded by those in church authority. Moreover, how could we have learned to participate more fully both in church and secular society as long as we were told to respect uncritically any kind of authority which presented itself to us? It is therefore high time that we break out of this web of self-asserting authority structures and equip ourselves spiritually, theologically and politically with the necessary information and strategies in order to re-enter both realms as actively as possible.

Hence before we can even begin to offer Christian contributions to political debates, we must think through in what it is exactly that our own Christian vision consists, that vision which we would like to offer to the wider human conversation on the meaning and future of our universe.

2.3 A Christian vision of the whole

In this section I wish to address the question of how we can articulate a Christian vision of the whole. That is a necessary step to be taken before we can proceed to a deliberation of concrete proposals for Christian faith-praxis in today's world. In the previous chapter we reflected upon Christ's proclamation of God's kingdom in this world. Now we have seen that this kingdom is not to be split in two halves, rather it is God's will that his kingdom is to be established here and now in our midst. We have seen above that the features of this kingdom include the freedom from all kinds of oppression, the radical equality to serve, and the element of surprise. But in light of what we have discussed just now in terms of God's care for this universe, we have to develop our characterisation of God's kingdom yet further.

If God cares for this world any consideration of his reign must include such matters as the environment, economics and politics. The environment is important as the physical context of God's kingdom. Economics is important because it offers reflections both on one important aspect of our relationship to each other and on how we are distributing the fruits of God's earth. And politics is important here in terms of how we are organising human life in this world and what structures of participation and authority we are setting up in order to enable human beings to relate properly to each other, to nature, to God and to themselves.

While it seems relatively easy to include our environment in our treatment of God's kingdom, economics and politics complicate the case significantly. Our Christian tradition has much to say about the world as God's creation and therefore implicitly also about how we ought to be treating this gift of God. But our tradition has many things – and even contradictory things – to say about how we are to organise authority and communal organisations both in the church and in the public social realm. No simple reference to tradition will therefore suffice here. Instead we need to develop our overall vision of the world and then assess again and again what strategies we may develop in order to work towards the realisation of that vision. However, since we saw already that this vision contains an element of divine surprise we must never come up with a closed vision which would keep God at bay rather than letting him in in order to transform our lives.

The vision which a critical reading of the biblical texts suggests is a vision of creative harmony between all people and all things. This harmony is never static, but dynamic, and that means it takes proper account of our temporality and mortality. If we are participating in a creative project, our own participation happens in time and space, and there is a time for letting go and handing over to others. What this means for the individual we shall consider in the next chapter. Here, however, it is important to state, however provisionally, our overall vision of the whole.

As Christians we see that God's project can unfold itself only with our invited help and never against it. The surprises with which we may have to reckon in our response to God's invitation are not nasty ones in the sense that God would pull our leg at times, rather the surprises of which we repeatedly spoke are good surprises. By this I mean, that whenever we are doing the will of God, things begin to happen in unexpected ways: we begin to see the world and our relationships differently and we are then not clinging any longer to our own limited view of the universe, instead we become open to the enlarging of our vision. Thus, our Christian vision of the whole cannot be static but has to be dynamic. We do not know all, but we know some important features of how to relate to God, to his creation, and this includes how to relate to our fellow human beings and to ourselves.

If we are to treat every human being, not just every self-confessed Christian, as being equally loved by God; in other words, if we are serious about human equality, then our Christian vision of the whole must never be oppressive, but should at best be suggestive. We can suggest modes of looking at and participating in this world, and we can suggest adequate ways of exercising political and economic power in this world. But we must resist those modes of private and public relationships which clearly lead to new inequalities, oppressions and manipulations.

The reader may feel that this is a rather incomplete vision – and it is indeed. Because we are involved not in implementing a Christian blueprint of the world, but in developing new and creative ways of relating to God, to his creation, to one another, and to ourselves, our vision can only be very sketchy and fragmentary. It is, if you like, a preliminary vision, since by definition it must remain open to new divine surprises. God's kingdom then is not a political programme, but it says something on how political programmes ought to proceed and what kind of view of the human being and of the environment they ought to facilitate.

Our vision of the whole is not completed – but we do have a vision, one which invites all people to participate, and a vision that God is present whenever we are involved in truly participatory activity in and on behalf of his creation. For instance, with regard to specific economic programmes and theories, our Christian vision must remain very critical of all those projects which do not allow *all* people to participate. Christians cannot accept what is often called a 'two-third-society'. That means we can never be satisfied with the fact that one third of a society will inevitably be excluded from the process of personal, social, cultural, political and economic development and public decision making. Similarly, monarchical and oligarchical structures of government inside or outside the church are not in accordance with the Christian vision since they will by necessity rule out the fair and equal participation of all.

Thus, we Christians understand God's creative project

in terms of a movement towards a participatory
community between human beings and God, which
allows all life to unfold its divinely inspired development.
The Jews call such a state of dynamic harmony 'shalom',
we Christians refer to it with the help of a number of
names such as 'kingdom of God', 'eternal life', and
'paradise'.

But what about the needs of the individual in all this?
We still have to die and we often suffer and feel excluded
from various aspects of life, at times even from
manifestations of Christian community. How does our
Christian faith allow a dynamic development of a vision
of the individual?

2.4 A Christian vision of individual participation in God's project

I am a mortal person. Nobody can take my death from
me. In a strange way one could argue that the fact of my
own death gives me a certain identity as an individual.
But it is a mortal identity, because it points to the fact of
my no longer being here. So why should I ultimately care
so much for this world since I am going to be removed
from it anyway sooner rather than later?

The answers given to this question vary significantly,
even within the Christian movement. There are those
who look for ways of securing 'life' after death. There are
those who have organised an entire symbolic universe for
the afterlife including heaven, hell, purgatory and limbo,
although there is no hint of the actual existence of such
structures in any of our foundational experiences or texts.
It is pure speculation, and in many ways a rather
unchristian speculation since it wishes to prescribe to
God that even after our life is over there should be no

divine surprises. However, I am afraid we will have to face up to God's privilege to surprise us. It is impossible to let God be all in all and at the same time to reduce him to the state of a puppet of our dreams of fear, uncertainty and anxiety. I shall treat of the Christian understanding of death and new life in more detail in the following chapter.

But in the context of this chapter it is important to see that, like Jesus Christ, we must learn to accept our death and the loneliness which goes with dying. We have hope, not because we have invested in a spiritual life-assurance policy which covers death, but because we have accepted our God-given life as a project and a responsibility within the larger project of God's creation. God's project then is larger than any individual life, but never less than appreciative of and protective of every single human life. The Irish description of a handicapped person as God's own person (*duine le Dia*) is a good illustration of that point. Old life, injured life, handicapped life: every life is God's own life, God's special gift and task.

Hence, there is no competition or conflict between the two visions, the one of the whole, and the one of my individual participation in God's overall project. Rather there is this added dignity that God's own project is linked to each and every individual response to it. God has willed not to develop this great project alone, but with our help and participation. What more could we want in terms of divine promise and appreciation?

In the light of these remarks we can now turn to a more balanced consideration of our chief concern in this chapter, namely how to build the faith community in response to God's invitation.

2.5 Building the faith community

In this section I would like to discuss three related issues: the purpose of Christian community, the nature of community, and the question of the distinction and connection between the two related aims of Christian life, i.e. love of God and love of neighbour.

2.5.1 THE PURPOSE OF CHRISTIAN COMMUNITY

The Christian community is involved in three activities, which must not be separated, but distinguished. We *proclaim* the new life, we *celebrate* the new life, and we *share* the new life.[2] In our proclamation we are first of all remembering the creative and redemptive presence of God in this world, e.g. the history of Israel, the person of Jesus Christ, the Christian tradition, and every life (past, present and future) in this universe. In our celebration we express in many different ways the joy of living and developing our life in God's presence. And the aspect of sharing our gift of new life with all others who have not been able for whatever reason to experience God's healing and reconciling presence points to the third dimension of our Christian community.

Thus, we can say that the purpose of Christian community is to manifest in different ways the relationship to which God has called us in his universe. This relationship is a life-affirming relationship and therefore interested in overcoming any reduction of life and any form of death. At the same time, this relationship with God does concern the entire universe. It is not a purely private or sectarian or separatist relationship, but it is open, universal in aspiration and inclusive. Therefore it calls for a steadily growing form of community, for a form of expressing in words, joyful celebration and emancipatory action that God has called every one of us to participate together in his great creative project.

2.5.2 THE NATURE OF CHRISTIAN COMMUNITY

That Christian faith calls for a communitarian response to God's invitation has become sufficiently clear by now. If God has invited all human beings to co-operate with him in his creative project we must respect each other's dignity as fellow workers. But that is more easily stated than practised. In fact anybody with some experience of church work will know only too well that conflicts are a routine feature of all Christian organisations and committees. Such conflicts about which way to respond to needs in concrete situations are, of course, a feature of all human organisation, but they are often even harsher in religious contexts where everybody feels ultimately and radically competent. Thus, it seems that it is even more difficult to arrive at some form of mutual understanding when sacred matters are involved. And that may be why we Christians have such a sad record of internal Christian fights and why there is such a high level of casualties arising from internal Christian disputes. It appears that we have a hard time recognising that God has given us often very different talents and that it takes time and patience to listen to the other as other and to encourage the other to develop and manifest his or her talents, even if this includes that I myself question my own approach to the transformation of this world towards God's kingdom. We Christians have a hard time coming to terms with otherness, and that on many levels.

2.5.3 THE DIFFICULTY WITH OTHERNESS

We have a hard time accepting the other in our own community, we have a hard time accepting that there are other Christian churches, and we have a hard time coming to terms with the fact that there are radically other ways of searching for the divine mysteries, i.e. the other world religions. But I also have a hard time in coming to terms with the other in my own self. That is to say, we encounter otherness on many levels of our experience at once. Otherness is always a challenge to our most cherished assumptions; it is a threat to what we have taken for granted so far, it makes us insecure and lets the world appear as a chaos rather than as an ordered whole in which we would be more readily at ease. However, given our insights into God's mysterious presence in our midst, we have to admit that God is the ultimate and radical other who undermines, as we have seen, with his surprising presence all of our firmly held views, convictions and visions. Therefore, the way in which we treat the other in our own midst is a good test of our willingness to reckon with God's radical otherness.

The following questions impose themselves in this context: Am I prepared to accept that there are other experiences of God's presence than my own? Am I prepared to consider other ways of understanding God's presence in Christ? Am I prepared to face the other in me? If the answer to these questions is 'No' then I have ruled out the possibility of relating adequately to God's mysterious presence in our world.

Thus, it is easy to demand a better Christian community, but very difficult to live up to the most basic requirement of any real or authentic community of fellow God-lovers. It is equally easy to say that God is a mystery, but very difficult to open oneself to this mysterious and radically other in our midst. But what is very clear is that we need each other to remind each other of the need to be open to each other and to God's radical otherness. Maybe we could learn here from Buddhists who argue that we ought not to cling to any understanding of any reality, even the reality of God, but we must let go if we really want to be renewed.

Christian faith demands a dynamic community and the participation of all Christians in this community. Hence, we must try and establish adequate structures in that community which facilitate each member's participation in the communal project of responding to God's call. However, participation requires training and preparation, and I therefore conclude this chapter by pointing to two of the ways in which this preparation can be achieved.

2.5.4 THE NEED FOR PROPER EDUCATION

First of all, each member of the Christian community must be given the possibility of a thorough education which enables her or him to discern with others – but if need be also critical of others – what are the central aspirations of the Christian community. This education must include proper information about the resources of Christian faith. Every Christian needs to be made familiar with the nature of the biblical texts, the possibilities of biblical interpretation, the ambiguous history of the Christian movement and of other religious movements, the spiritual masters of the Christian tradition, and the basic theological tools which enable Christians to listen, reflect, think and assess for themselves what is required from them in order to respond most adequately to God's call in Christ. In other words, every Christian must be prepared to search afresh for the presence of God in the different contexts of this world.

Obviously, such an education in Christian faith

presupposes a basic level of literacy. For this reason too, Christians need to help in the fight against illiteracy.

2.5.5 LOVE OF GOD AND LOVE OF NEIGHBOUR

Understanding and responding to the radical otherness of God requires training in tackling all forms of otherness. To demand that we Christians have to become more pluralistic in our attitudes is only a beginning. What we have ultimately to strive for is the openness to encounter God's ultimate challenge of our understanding and self-understanding in many more ways than we have seen necessary before.

We must learn how to distinguish between love of God and love of neighbour without separating the two from each other. Matthew 22 makes quite clear that we cannot love God without loving our neighbour, but it stresses with equal force that love of God is not the same as love of neighbour. We must learn to love God for God's own sake. However, this we will never be able to do if we are not prepared to love our neighbour for her or his own sake. Human charity, human concern for other humans and for the universe as a whole is important, but it is not the final aim of Christians. Rather, the ultimate aim of Christians is to love God or, to say it more modestly, to learn how to love God for God's own sake. This learning experience is what Christian life is ultimately about. We are not yet God-lovers as such by attending lovingly to the needs of the poor, oppressed, marginalised, and the needs of an exploited nature. Everybody can engage in these activities without subscribing to faith in the God of Israel and Jesus Christ. Rather, as the great Christian mystics have taught us, our desire to know more about God will automatically point us to God's creative project and to the various needs of this project. If we attend to all the needs around us without this desire of loving God, we may be in danger of confusing our perception of what needs to be done with the real needs of God's project; we may be in danger of confusing ourselves with God. However, a genuine willingness to find out more about God and his project will provide us with a more critical perspective on our limited personal calling to listen, understand and respond to God's own plan.

Looking at the vocation stories of many prophetic figures in Israel's or the Christian movement's history, we can observe that God calls those people, who, such as Moses, are compassionate, willing to engage in emancipatory action and fight for people's freedom to relate properly to God, each other and the world. But it is interesting to see how this desire to do God's work needs to be purified again and again. The burning-bush experience of Moses (Exodus 3) may be a fitting symbol for our own need to have our most sacred desires purified in the test of our personal relationship to God. The entire network of relationships, that is my love for God, my neighbour, God's creation and for myself, may be transformed by the fire of God's love for me. Similarly, Jesus had to undergo the desert experience in order to test his calling before embarking on his public ministry. Are we prepared to face the desert with the demons of self-delusion and rivalry with God in order to prepare ourselves for our ministry in response to God's call?

2.6 Conclusion

In this chapter we have continued our reflection on our vocation to respond to God's invitation to establish his kingdom in our midst. We have seen that proclaiming, celebrating and sharing the good news of God's kingdom are the purpose of Christian community. We have discussed the danger of splitting our everyday world from God's creative project. But we have also become aware of some of the difficulties which need to be confronted when we engage in building the faith community.

The most radical challenge, however, of every effort to respond to God's call is our understanding of the certain fact of our death. What is the point of my contribution to the building of a faith community when I am dying anyway? Is death then the ultimate enemy of Christian faith-praxis? We have to address these questions first before we can proceed to explore our individual and communal responses to God's call. But by doing so we are on our way to penetrate some aspects of God's radical and creative mystery.

3

DEATH AND LIFE IN JESUS CHRIST

3.0 Introduction

It may appear somewhat morbid that I propose to tackle the question of death at this point in our discussion of our response to God's call. Why death in the middle of our reflection on the nature and purpose of Christian community?

The answer to this question seems relatively simple: If our Christian commitment and our individual and communal hopes and visions cannot pass the test of the awareness of our death, they are not worth living for. Thus, all of what we have considered so far ought to be looked at again in view of the fact that we are all going to die sooner or later, each one of us. Yet this test of our hopes, visions and plans in the light of our certain death is not as easy and straightforward as one might think. Our death, though a certain fact, is not a reality to which we find it easy to relate. Moreover, strangely enough, some of our own Christian hopes have helped to alter the appearance of death to us, and thus have taken away from death as the ultimate challenge to our hopes. I shall have to explain this paradox during this chapter.

Until the advent of materialism in the nineteenth century few people really believed that their death was in fact the end of their personal career. Rather death was taken to be the important point in every individual's journey where body and soul were separated. Death as the total end to a human journey was a perception shared neither by the builders of the hill tombs in Ireland, for instance at Newgrange, nor by the Greeks, nor indeed by our Christian ancestors. In all known cultures the dead were believed to have some place where they could rest and join with other dead, be these places good or bad or (as in many of the texts of the Hebrew Scriptures) as yet unspecified. In fact, it is striking that the Hebrew Scriptures (that is for Christians the Old Testament), on the whole, do not promote any concrete hopes for the dead other than to say that their biological existence has ended, that the event of death has separated the dead from the living. While the living can still praise God, 'the dead do not praise the Lord, nor do any that go down into silence' (Ps. 115:17).

Over against the shadow existence of the dead in Hebrew thought, the early Christians proclaimed the resurrection of the dead. Jesus of Nazareth's resurrection from the dead was seen by the apostle Paul as the beginning of a new order. Paul explains as follows:

> *Now if Christ is proclaimed as raised from the dead, how can some of you say there is no resurrection of the dead? If there is no resurrection of the dead, then Christ has not been raised; and if Christ has not been raised, then our proclamation has been in vain and your faith has been in vain. We are even found to be misrepresenting God, because we testified of God that he raised Christ – whom he did not raise if it is true that the dead are not raised. For if the dead are not raised, then Christ has not been raised. If Christ has not been raised, your faith is futile and you are still in your sins. Then those also who have died in Christ have perished. If for this life only we have hoped in Christ, we are of all people most to be pitied.*
> (1 Cor. 15:12–19).

And Paul concludes his reflections on resurrection

> *When this perishable body puts on imperishability,
> and this mortal body puts on immortality, then the
> saying that is written [in the Hebrew Scriptures] will
> be fulfilled: 'Death has been swallowed up in victory.'
> 'Where, O death, is your victory? Where, O death, is
> your sting?'* (1 Cor. 15:54–5).

Thus, Paul saw the prophecies of Isaiah (25:8) and Hosea (13:14) now as fulfilled: death is destroyed for ever.

However, Paul died and all disciples of Christ since have also died exactly like all other mortals on this globe have done. Obviously, Jesus has not delivered biological immortality to us. The struggle with physical death continues, and all manifestations of physical death continue to hurt us deeply. Thus, reflection on the unavoidability of physical death is not a sign of the sinful or the infidel, rather it is an important activity for the Christian believer. Our life is limited by death. We ought to take this limit very seriously and attempt to come to terms with it as best we can. But just that seems more difficult today than ever before.

3.1 Contemporary culture and death: the illusion of immortality

In one way we may seem to be much more closely acquainted today with the reality of death than any generation before us, and yet to some extent, we and especially those of us who live in bigger cities are increasingly out of touch with death. Let me explain this paradox.

The emergence of mass communication has made it possible for us to witness death more or less continuously on our television screens. Somewhere in the world spectacular death happens at any given time and we can participate almost immediately and sometimes even 'live' in this spectacle via telecommunication. However, at the same time we have got used to the portrayal of death as a routine cinematic event – with such a measure of success that the entire Western world can now mourn Bobby's death in the Australian soap opera 'Home and Away'. For my children Bobby's fictional death was more real than the tragic and untimely death in Germany of my cousin Susanne at the time of the Irish screening of Bobby's fictional death. And yet, Bobby's death is not really real, we know that we can switch off and change channel if we cannot bear the fact of her 'death'.

In contemporary suburbia the reality of death imposes itself on us very rarely, except perhaps when a member of our own immediate household dies. But in our big cities the number of people living in a household is rapidly falling. The effect of this development is that fewer and fewer people can be expected to have any direct experience of death in their immediate surroundings, in spite of the regular appearance of fictional or actual death on their television screen. From the latter experience, however, we can switch off when we do not like its presence. Thus, paradoxically, the retreat of death from our awareness is promoted by the very medium which nowadays paints it so colourfully on the screen.

Moreover, lots of screen experiences suggest immortality. Mickey Mouse celebrates one birthday and triumph after the other, yet never ages. Coca Cola and Pepsi Cola are as young as ever. Captain Scarlet does not die; Flipper still swims; and Richard Kimble relives again his escape from police custody. The new computer games provide three, seven, twelve and more 'lives' to each player. Real death is rarely brought home to us, and as a result of this fact we are less and less prepared to face it when we grow older. The often neurotic relationship to death is a direct result of this inability among younger people to learn how to face death. Whole industries are busy now removing the last traces of death from our midst. Death is, on the whole, good neither for business nor for the contemporary imagination promoted in some measure by business interests. To quote my colleague Gabriel Daly, 'A world without faith is likely to be a world that is oppressed by the prospect of death. . . . The best that a faithless world can do with death is to regard it as an obscenity and repress it as far as possible.'[1]

The old and famous tradition of the Irish wake is now fast disappearing. 'Indecorous many a wake may have been, but by making death a familiar it prevented repression and gave social expression to a faith which affirms the transience not only of life *but also of death* ... There is something of it still found in the general Irish attitude to death, but one cannot help wondering how much of it will survive advancing urbanisation and secularisation, which affects the unconscious attitudes of believers as well as unbelievers.'[2]

More and more, especially in larger urban areas, we ban real death from our homes as much as we can and relocate it to the clinical atmosphere of our high-tech hospitals. As a result death appears often to be a failure of medicine and science, as if these disciplines were responsible for the general set-up of human life and its definite limitations. And if death should still surprise us at home our corpses are quickly removed to funeral 'homes' by their well-trained staff. Hence, death which we cannot control is banned from our attention as far as possible, while only death which we can master by remote control is allowed to enter our consciousness. Even when we allow ourselves to hear of millions of deaths in Somalia, Angola, Rwanda, Sudan and Yugoslavia we have hardly a chance of properly relating to such an item of bad news because we largely have lost access to the mystery of our own mortality and death. These days it is much more difficult to prove our mortality than our immortality.[3]

Even our linguistic treatment of death witnesses to our uneasiness of coping with the fact of death. We tend to refer to the 'passing' of a loved one; we mention those who 'can no longer be with us'. But rarely do we refer explicitly to the brutal fact of somebody's death. In many Christian quarters we pray for the souls of the deceased and articulate our belief that although their bodily existence is finished, their life may continue uninterrupt-edly now carried on by the soul. Hence, the dead are dead, but not fully. Their death is restricted only to the biological circumstances of their life story.

My thesis is that vital horizons for the human understanding of death and life are lost when human death is understood only as the not-so-nice passage of the soul, separated now from the body, to one or another form of immortality. For people firmly rooted in this body–soul separation, death ceases to represent a radical challenge. In opposition to such people I believe that in order to reconstruct an adequate Christian theory of life and even eternal life in Christ, we first of all ought to face up better or more fully to the experience of death which lies ahead of each one of us.

3.2 The phenomenon of death

None of us still alive has ever experienced physical or
biological death. And even those who every so often
come forward to talk to us about their very personal near-
to-death experiences have come back to life and thus
have not really experienced death, but begun to
experience the process of dying. Dying, however, is still
part of life. Only when the dying ends, does death occur.

Interestingly enough, there is still some controversy
among scientists about the most accurate way of defining
the death of a person: heart death, brain death, lung
death, and psychogenic death figure among the most
usual references in this debate on the criteria for clinical
death, a debate which has recently received new urgency
in view of the need to know when a person is dead
enough so as to permit the removal of his or her organs
for transplantation. This debate need not concern us here.
For our purpose it is sufficient to state that death has
arrived when all biological activity in a person has come
to an end and the process of active decomposition sets in.
What must concern us, however, is the question of how
dead is dead?

At this point is may be useful to remember that there is
a second level of language about death. We refer to
somebody still fully alive and state that he or she is dead
for us. By this we mean that we do not wish to entertain
any communication with such a person. One could speak
of this phenomenon as 'social death'. There are lots of
examples of social death in our respective contexts. But
there are also the experiences and related expressions of
other forms of death, such as psychological death,
ecological death, linguistic death, divine death and even
spiritual death. Spiritual death is that which the Jewish

and Christian traditions call the death caused by sin. What all of these experiences of partial death have in common is that a set of relationships has been profoundly disturbed so that it makes sense metaphorically to call somebody dead who is biologically still alive. Here our experience of somebody's physical death has been used in order to speak metaphorically of the breakdown of a particular set of relationships, inter-human, divine-human, or – as in the case of psychological death – the relationship of a person to his or her own self.

These observations show that we experience the phenomenon of death generally in terms of destruction of relationships. However, the qualitative difference between these partial experiences of death and the event of death as the end of one's life is that the former so-called 'deaths' can be undone, but not so the latter. Death at the end of a life's journey is irreversible. And even the biblical belief in resurrection never aims at undoing death. We shall have to come back to this point in a moment.

Death as the physical limit to our existence means the irrevocable breakdown of *all* actual and possible relationships in which we have been or can be actively involved. To us the living, the dead remain dead, out of bounds, and all of our efforts to imagine what may have happened to them in death are but efforts to interpret in mythological terms what death could mean or what we would like it to mean. The truth of this matter is that we just do not know and cannot know what comes after death. It is crucial that we admit that we actually *cannot* know or influence death and its particularities, precisely because we are still alive. And as long as we are alive we share in the limitations imposed on us by space, time and language. These limitations only lose their significance in death. Therefore we can only escape from their limiting power at the price of death.

Why is it so difficult for us to accept these limitations which life imposes on us? Why do we wish to rule beyond life? Why, when facing death, can we often not easily let go and commit ourselves into the hands of a faithful God? Is it because we lack faith in God, or is it that our faith has been more or less systematically misguided by many of the spokespersons of our own Christian tradition? We come back to these questions later in this chapter. Here, however, it is important that we honestly admit that we really do not know and, by definition, cannot know anything about our death as long as we are alive. But this does not mean that we should not think and talk about the meaning of our death for our lives. Rather it means that we should acknowledge the mysterious nature of our death already here and now.

The language of heaven, hell, purgatory and limbo is fully mythological and, as Jean-Paul Sartre observed some time ago in his play *Huis Clos*, says usually more about how we relate to our neighbours than what we actually believe will happen to us ourselves. Images of so-called life after death are the fruits of our imagination and not the result of verifiable experience. They may have their value as symbolic expressions of our present relationship to God, each other and ourselves, but these images ought not to be understood as the signposts of a supernatural geography needed for our eternal journey. In this regard I can only agree with the German philosopher Walter Schulz's verdict that we can no longer meaningfully live by the metaphysical concepts of continued existence and personal immortality. Rather we must accept the biologically orientated concept of natural death.[4]

3.3 A theology of natural death

Since Friedrich Schleiermacher's time early in the nineteenth century a number of Protestant theologians have defended the thesis that the death of a person marks the end of all actual relations. This thesis is at times referred to as the theory of total death.[5] Eberhard Jüngel, for instance, defines death as the impossibility of proper relatedness.[6] By this he means that death puts the limit to all of our own efforts to establish proper relationships. In this context he strongly denies an immortality of the human soul.[7] Death puts an end to all life of a person. What remains is God's act of love in our death. God has limited human life through death. Where we become totally powerless in death, God becomes power-full.[8] Where we cannot do anything any longer, God is there for us. Thus, what remains alone in our death is God's faithfulness to us without any carrier of the divine–human relationship on our side. In our death God is all in all.

Jüngel urges us to distinguish sharply between natural death and untimely or unnatural death. Natural death must be accepted as our God-ordained natural boundary. Biologists say that the normal life-span of a man is about eighty years, and that of a woman about eighty-five years. Untimely death, however, must never be accepted as ordained by God and therefore must be fought precisely because it offends against the God-given life-span.

Following one major trend in Christian theology Jüngel draws also a distinction between death as natural event and death as curse of the sinner. This distinction guides Jüngel's interpretation of St Paul's references to death as the wages of sin, especially in his Letter to the Romans (Rom. 6:23). Jüngel argues that normal death becomes such a threat to us, because faced with death we appreciate the sinfulness of our lives and that means the brokenness of our relationships, especially our relationship with God.

This kind of theological approach to death stands in considerable contrast to statements by the Roman Catholic Magisterium. Over the centuries the church has repeatedly claimed that death is the result of human sinfulness.

3.4 Death as the result of Adam's sin?

While many prominent Protestant theologians have warned against a dualistic approach to the mystery of death, statements by the Roman Catholic Magisterium have stressed not only the body–soul separation at the point of death, but also the view that even biological death has been caused by Adam's sinfulness. The most recent expression of these views can be found in the new *Catechism of the Catholic Church.*[9]

The *Catechism* states clearly that 'Death is the end of earthly life.' (§1007). As such it gives our life some urgency. We do not have unlimited time for the realisation of our life. But in the paragraph immediately following here the *Catechism* defines:

> *Death is a consequence of sin. The Church's Magisterium, as authentic interpreter of the affirmations of Scripture and Tradition, teaches that death entered the world on account of man's sin. Even though man's nature is mortal, God had destined him not to die. Death was therefore contrary to the plans of God the Creator, and entered the world*

as a consequence of sin. 'Bodily death, from which
man would have been immune had he not sinned' is
thus 'the last enemy' of man to be conquered.
(§1008)[10]

I have quoted the entire paragraph 1008 in order to
document that the *Catechism* restates with great clarity
that death has entered God's creation because of human
sin. Moreover, already in the *Catechism*'s treatment of the
doctrine of original sin, this interpretation was put
forward (§§400–409). The *Catechism* refers to Romans
5:12 as the biblical foundation for this assessment of the
origin of death:

> *Therefore, just as sin came into the world through*
> *one man, and death came through sin, and so death*
> *spread to all because all have sinned.*

Following the second Council of Orange in 529 and the
Council of Trent in the sixteenth century, the literal
reading of this Pauline passage has thus once more been
applied as the foundation for this dualistic approach to
death. Death comes to focus here not as the natural end
to our life as ordained by God, but as punishment.
Hence, the natural conditions of our life are seen as
ultimately not originating in God's will, but as a
consequence of our rejection of God's will. Moreover, it
is striking to observe what kind of image of God is
proposed here. It is a God who is involved in continuous
punishment of all human beings. This perspective on
God is not compatible with the God preached by Jesus of
Nazareth. Nor is this interpretation of Romans 5:12
adequate.

As we have seen already above, as in 1 Corinthians so
also here St Paul refers to death metaphorically in order

to describe the nature of sin, i.e. our broken relationship with God. 'Death' used in this context is indeed the wages of sin. But Paul never questions the fact that the natural condition in which we live was ordained by God. He never considers the origins of natural death. Rather he takes the natural conditions and limitations of life so much for granted that he insists in 1 Corinthians 15 that even those who might still be alive when Christ comes again are in need of being transformed radically. 'We will not all die, but we will all be changed, in a moment, in the twinkling of an eye, at the last trumpet.' (1 Cor.15:51f.). However, Paul interprets all forms of death in the light of the experience of Christ's resurrection, an experience which makes sense only as long as Jesus was thought to have really died. In this regard it is also of interest to remember that neither Jesus nor any of his disciples, nor Paul, ever talked about a body–soul split in death whereby the soul would act as a carrier for the continuation of life. This body–soul dualism which infiltrated Christian thinking very early in the post-apostolic period originates in Greek philosophy and Gnostic speculation and is incompatible both with the strong materialism underlying the accounts of Jesus's death and with the accounts of Jesus's resurrection in the gospels.

The official Roman Catholic theology of death is, unfortunately, intrinsically flawed. It neither takes death as the God-ordained boundary to human life seriously, nor does it consider death as a comprehensive and total end to human power. Rather it holds human beings in general responsible for death and proclaims God as the one who, with the help of the church's sacraments and hierarchy, promises the eventual undoing of his own awful verdict on humankind. It must also be said that this kind of theology is methodologically untenable because it firstly reduces the Bible to a reservoir of literal proof-texts for basically unbiblical attitudes towards death, and secondly negates the foundational experience that all living beings have only a limited life-span. This denial of the basic human experience of nature does not encourage trust in the overall competence of this theological perspective and it runs the risk of fundamentally discouraging the careful study of other aspects of the teaching of the Vatican in the new *Catechism* or elsewhere which may be genuinely more promising.

It is sad that the countless warnings by prominent theologians, including Roman Catholic ones, during the last few decades were ignored once again, and an old and fundamentally non-Christian doctrine of death was reaffirmed. The late Karl Rahner, for instance, with uncharacteristic clarity repeatedly stressed that death is the natural experience of the end of our life. 'With death the one history of the human being ceases once and for all.'[11] Death is a natural phenomenon which is as such not dependent on 'Adam'. With much greater clarity than the new *Catechism*, Rahner analysed that as Christians we human beings never experience death only as a natural phenomenon. Rather we experience death as a multifaceted phenomenon whose dimensions include the natural aspect, but also the personal aspect of possible guilt and sin, precisely because the spectre of our death forces us to consider the complexity of our relationships, and exposes especially our relationship to God.

Though in principle Rahner maintains the distinction between body and soul, he qualifies the definition of death as the split of the two and thus moves closer towards an understanding of the comprehensiveness of death. 'Death is an event that concerns the entire human being.'[12]

The reader may wonder why I am so determined to defend the experience of death as first and foremost a natural experience, not caused by sin and never undone by God's saving action in Christ. The reason is this: I consider the biological dimension of our death vital for any serious discussion of the personal, i.e. existential, attitude to our death. Moreover, I consider the biological dimension of our death vital for any adequate approach to the death and resurrection of Jesus of Nazareth as the foundation for our hope in eternal life.

3.5 The death and resurrection of Jesus of Nazareth

It is not the task of the Christian theologian to explain the mystery of death as such, but to interpret the meaning of human death in view of the life, death and resurrection of Jesus Christ.

Jesus died desolate on the cross, and he really died. The awful circumstances of his death must always be recalled when we speak about the glory of his resurrection. Moreover, it is a crucial element of most reports on the presence of the risen Christ to point to his wounds and thus the circumstances of his death. Jesus was really and comprehensively dead. His death was never undone. Resurrection does not mean that death, after all, was not quite so bad, or that the soul of Jesus enjoyed a God-given escape in death. Rather, resurrection as a gracious act of God is only possible once all human freedom and power have come to a complete and irreversible end in death. The materialistic attitude to the death of Jesus present in all the gospels cannot be overemphasised against the background of the theory of body–soul separation. Jesus was really dead and therefore not in a position to save himself. His life ended prematurely, tragically. His cruel death seen in isolation can never be considered as the will of God. Rather Jesus maintained his total commitment to God's will even when he faced the certainty of his personal extinction. Thus, even the just, the one who does the will of the Father, suffered death. In raising Jesus from the dead God has not undone the laws of nature; rather he has manifested his faithfulness to his son both by accepting the total self-giving and accompanying powerlessness of Jesus on the cross and by glorifying Jesus as the first-born of a new eternal order of relationships as they should be.

The resurrection of Jesus is a mystery, not a secret. That is to say that, though we cannot abstractly reveal its essence, we can allow ourselves to be drawn into it by following Jesus. As long, however, as we insist on carrying a certain amount of spiritual baggage with us beyond our life, as long as we, so to speak, prepare our stamp collection for eternal inspection, as long as we expect to be carried to eternity on the wings of a well-groomed soul, we have missed the point of Jesus's death and resurrection. And most disturbingly, we have missed the point of our own life and death. It is dangerous for our life to speak carelessly about our death.[13] And as long as we do not take seriously the totality of our death, we cannot really begin to enter the mystery of Jesus's resurrection.

Jesus did not free us either from death or from the need to live a life marked by the urgency of death. Rather he freed us from the neurotic fear of death, from the anxiety of a life ending in sinful distance from God, and he freed us for a life of freedom and creativity in God's presence. Moreover, Jesus's own destiny has shown that our life matters to God, so much so that in his mysterious ways God is committed to each one of us by promising to raise us to eternal life in his glorious presence. No image can ever hope to grasp the fullness of this mystery of resurrection. Maybe one should grant that even the old soul-language tried, however badly, to express something of this resurrection hope. The all-important question surely is this: Does God seek to have continuous contact with me beyond the event of my own radical contingency? Since there can be no human image ever to describe this continuity in discontinuity we have to use the best of dialectical expression to state what we believe and, at the same time, to put a question mark beyond any chosen statement.

The hope emerging for us from Jesus Christ's resurrection does not concern any belief in immortality, nor any form of guarantee of uninterrupted continuity for us. Rather, as St Paul underlined vigorously, the hope for us made possible as a result of the resurrection of Christ builds on God's ultimate faithfulness and his eternal will to establish a lasting relationship with us. In this sense John can say that God is love (1 John 4:8). The only important question for us then is whether we wish to respond to this offer made in Jesus Christ and, if our response is 'Yes', how.

3.6 Death and Christian hope

In his famous work *Being and Time* (1927), the German philosopher Martin Heidegger analysed the possibilities of human existence which are opened up by an honest awareness of our human mortality.[14] From a Christian viewpoint this honest approach to the certainty of our death must be welcomed. But the freedom which Heidegger discovers as forthcoming from his reflection on death does not satisfy the Christian believer. Not to escape from the reality of natural death is one thing, to see death in the horizon of Christian experience is another. The difference is significant.

For the philosopher death becomes the methodological point of departure for adequate human reflection and action; for the Christian believer death is much more challenging. Death is the ultimate challenge to all of our material and concrete hopes, actions and aspirations. Death is even the ultimate challenge to all of our views of God. This latter insight, so carefully developed by the best Christian mystics, emphasises the human inability to say anything adequate about God's essence which would pass the challenge of our non-being. Unlike Heidegger, the Christian mystic knows that death is not the reservoir for life, but life is the reservoir for adequate ways of dying. As the point of radical self-abandonment, death could become even attractive, not as a quick fix to the nightmare of life, but as an ultimate emptiness to be filled totally by God. Death in this sense, however, needs a life-long preparation, a strenuous discipline of a life concerned with the mystery of God. Death in this sense has absolutely nothing to do with morbid feeling or thinking. Rather it becomes the paradigm for new creation, new life, eternal life.

St Paul contemplates these possibilities very carefully in his Letter to the Romans when he writes:

Do you not know that all of us who have been baptised into Christ Jesus were baptised into his death? Therefore we have been buried with him by baptism into death, so that, just as Christ was raised from the dead by the glory of the Father, so we too might walk in newness of life. (Rom. 6:3–4).

Paul's point here is not that the Christians in Rome whom he addresses, or indeed we today, have already physically died, which we clearly have not. Rather he encourages the Romans and ultimately us to take the experience of the totality of our physical death as an analogy for our need to allow God to fill this creative void so that we can begin to experience more and more fully God's presence and the newness of life in Christ. The New Testament texts state again and again Jesus's proclamation that eternal life starts here and now. It is the quality of God's relationship to us and God's faithfulness to us which awards us eternal life already here and now. Christian hope is therefore firmly rooted in this quality of divine–human relationship. It is the unmerited gift of this new quality of eternal relationship which we celebrate in the Eucharist. The Eucharist then is the occasion where all of our purified hopes, where our transition from death to life, our thankfulness for God's mysterious promise of resurrection are proclaimed, celebrated and shared. As such the Eucharist is our first and foremost experience of a proper relationship: with God, with each other, with nature and with ourselves. We shall reflect more upon this unique centre of Christian life in the following chapter.

So what can we as Christians faced with death realistically hope for? We can hope that our death is two things at once, namely the radical discontinuity of our life and a new opening, an opening to the consummation of a new relationship with God which has begun already in our life. Death is then the end of our life, but not an end in itself. As we have seen above, it is dangerous to imagine what lies beyond our death, because this endangers our view of life. On the other hand, we need images which are able to assert our hope that our individual life finds grace with God so that our individuality is received and resurrected by God in ways unknown to us. Saying too little about God's ultimate action on our behalf weakens our hope; saying too much weakens our faith in God. Thus, we need images and expressions of our ultimate hope and we must be grateful to all the artists who have tried to give expressions to this hope in words, painting, sculpture and music. We also need thoughts, even ontological and metaphysical efforts, of trying to express the ultimately unexpressable. Our problem, however, has been that occasionally we have believed in our own images and expressions, instead of believing with them in God's much greater reality.

3.7 Conclusion

In this chapter I have tried to show that Christian hope in eternal life has nothing to do with immortality; just the opposite is the case. Christian hope is based on the experience of God's action with the crucified Christ. Christian hope knows that resurrection does not mean the undoing of death. Rather the resurrection of Jesus of Nazareth shows us that God confirmed Jesus's particular life-story and his death in an unforeseen and surprising way. Thus God gave us all an example of his radical love for us, especially at the moment of our own absolute powerlessness. The belief in God's resurrecting action is foundational for any adequate Christian response to God's call. On the basis of this belief we can free ourselves from neurotic attitudes and actions with regard to our own death. Moreover, we can learn how to live with our death. In antiquity as well as in the Middle Ages it was a generally known slogan that the real art of life is the real art of dying. *Ars vivendi est ars moriendi.* We may have to retrieve this particular tradition and grasp afresh its deep wisdom. Then we may be able to make more realistic plans for our life, and for our life together. Then we will be freed to turn our attention to the building of our faith community, to the individual and communal response to God's call. Then we no longer need to hunt for securities of one sort or another which promise to guarantee our safe passage from the state of life to whatever comes beyond death. Then we are free to co-operate with God's creative project already here and now.

The sadness of seeing a friend or relative die will remain. The experience of death will leave its marks on all of us. But maybe we will learn how to integrate this experience into our life, rather than engaging in escapism and neurotic behaviour. It will not be easy for us to develop a constructive attitude towards the most destructive event in our life. We need the support and the witness of our Christian communities on our way towards nurturing such an attitude, particularly in view of the general denial of the reality of death in our young people's culture in the West. We need, in short, a new culture of dealing with the reality of death. As Christians we have no reason not to be involved in the development of such a culture, since we share the hope that the eternal life in which we pray to be resurrected has long begun.

4

EUCHARISTIC DISCIPLESHIP

4.0 Introduction

Where do we find the true church of Jesus Christ today? In South America where people are experiencing the good news of Christ as a message of liberation, a liberation from oppression by state terror and capitalist exploitation? In China or other oppressive contexts where Christians witness to their faith in the God of Jesus Christ in prison cells? Is the Christian community most alive in the slums of Calcutta where Mother Theresa shows the poorest of the poor that they are not forgotten, not totally deprived of human dignity in their desperate situation? Or can we locate the true church today in the poorest parts of Africa where Christians show that they really mean what they say when they try to follow Jesus by giving food and hope to the hungry, by burying the dead and by demonstrating human solidarity? And where can the true church be found in Europe or North America today? Should we look for it at huge Rock Festivals where people enjoy the community of listening to a Bob Geldof or U2 who are celebrating the joy of music and the show of solidarity with victims of hunger and war in the world? Or can we still find true Christian community and solidarity in the traditional churches of the affluent, but disorientated West? Do these Western congregations still listen to God's Word or do they chiefly administer what previous generations perceived to be God's Word? Or do they today only listen, but not respond to God's will?

These questions bring us back to the need for Christian reflection, that is to theology. For it is theology's task to think about God's revelation, about God's will and his promise of healing presence today. Theology is the rational account of Christian faith. Thus, it is charged with thinking about this world and about the Christian faith, and about what the two have to say to each other and where the two can meet.

In this chapter I outline what I perceive to be a critical and constructive understanding of the relationship of the Christian church to this world and to reflect upon the eucharistic character of Christian discipleship.

4.1 The church in the world

As we have seen in Chapter 1, the church is not the kingdom of God. Maybe this insight is described best in the words of Alfred Loisy: 'Jesus proclaimed the kingdom and it was the church that came.' This often-quoted sentence is usually interpreted to mean that the church is the disappointing reality of Christian existence in this world, and a clear sign that the reality of God's kingdom is still far away from us. One could, however, interpret the same sentence more positively and say: The church is the manifestation of our response to God's call in this world. Unfortunately, it is still far from God's kingdom, yet it sees itself as a network of communities who work together towards this kingdom. It lives in a state of tension between a presently incomplete manifestation and its future fulfilment. Or as Karl Barth saw it, it lives 'between the times'. The church exists no longer in a time without hope, it knows that God is present, yet it is unable fully to establish his kingdom on its own. Therefore it hopes and trusts that God will fulfil his promise of completing the process of the emergence of his kingdom.

This Christian hope, however, is not a passive hope. The opposite is the case. The life of the church between the times should mean that the church is totally concerned with preparing for God's time, that is with accepting the gift of God's kingdom. On this journey, the church is not left alone, because it moves under the guidance of God's Spirit, that is the Spirit of Jesus Christ. This Spirit helps us to assess critically and self-critically the role of the Christian church in this world. Therefore we must reflect upon the dimensions of this Spirit first. What is the Spirit of Jesus Christ?

Jesus was and always remained a Jew, a Jew fully devoted to God and committed to do God's will until the end of his life. This faith made him travel from Galilee to Jerusalem, this faith in the love of Israel's God which he proclaimed to everybody who cared to listen. Jesus clashed, however, with the Jewish religious authorities of his time, not because he would have dismissed out of hand the authority of Temple and Torah which every Jew was expected to respect. Rather he clashed because he had dared to *relativise* both religious authorities. Moreover he clashed because he had questioned the absoluteness of the value of the family and because he questioned the necessity of the ethnic quality of belonging to the Land of Israel for an adequate divine–human relationship. Even non-Jews are invited to enter into a proper relationship with the God of Israel. Jesus had put the love of God and of God's children first. The reign of God was his true concern, not the totalitarian or nationalist interpretations of the law and of the aspirations of other religious institutions. Jesus's attitudes were understood to be a threat by those people who placed their trust first and foremost in the proper functioning of these institutions while missing more and more of the original religious purpose and spiritual direction of these institutions. Given this description of Jesus in the gospels it would be a complete and tragic misunderstanding to claim that he, this same Jesus, intended to found yet another set of religious institutions.

4.2 Ambiguities

The story of Christianity is, as we all know, a story full of such tragic misunderstandings and strange ambiguities. In our Christian history we find institutions even worse than the totalitarian administration of Law and Temple. We find an inquisition who condemned people to death in the name of Jesus Christ. We find conquistadores who claimed the right to conquer people and continents in the name of Jesus Christ, while in reality they were mostly gold-hungry adventurers. We find many new laws and many new temples, all established in the name of Jesus, who have tyrannised the children of the God of love. The different temples, then, began to compete with one another, not only as to which of them most faithfully inquired into and then responded to God's creative will, but often, unfortunately, as to which of them was the more powerful politically and which of them preserved more successfully traditional ethnic and family values. Dubious politics were identified with the church of Jesus Christ, and to this day some of our politicians love to refer to the Christian church as a cheap provider of an authority that rules out any possible criticism of their unjust regimes.

Our reaction to these political distortions of church

should not lead us to demand that the Christian church stay out of politics altogether. Such advocacy of political innocence, which we can hear disturbingly often nowadays, is naive and wrong. As we have already seen in Chapter 2, Christian faith is deeply concerned with this world and therefore has also an intrinsic political dimension. Therefore it is important that we develop criteria which help us to assess the various contributions of Christian faith to the political realm, including our own.

The church is all of us, all of us who are in varying degrees unworthy disciples of Jesus Christ, all of us who seek an answer today to God's invitation issued to us in Jesus Christ. The church is not a metaphysical body of politically innocent 'angels', but the social reality of Christ's disciples in today's world. All of us who seek the Spirit of Jesus Christ as guidance on our journey towards God's kingdom are the church.

Of course, as disciples of Christ we stand in the tradition, the ambiguous tradition, of all the Christians who have attempted to follow Christ during these last twenty centuries. This tradition, however, is not a sacred reality in itself. Rather, it has to be examined with a critical eye. It calls for a continuous critical assessment of any of its hierarchical and other dimensions in the light of our understanding of Christ's Spirit.[1]

Yet too many Christians love a neatly defined hierarchical institution, because such an institution encourages them to transfer their individual and personal responsibility to this hierarchy. Either they find the hierarchy good, which allows them to think that all is well in God's church and that they themselves can relax in this secure feeling; or they dislike the hierarchy, which makes them feel that the entire church is just bad and there is nothing to be gained from personal involvement in it. And finally, there are those people who were formerly involved in the church, but who now want to maintain that the church is bound to remain as bad as when they 'rightly' left it. All three of these groups have a vested interest that there be no change or reform in the church.

A careful reading of the gospels informs us that Jesus did not transfer his personal responsibility as son of God on to the hierarchies of his time. Rather, he challenged those hierarchical institutions. He took his cross and followed God's call unto his awful death. But not only did he take his own cross, he also encouraged others to do the same. His confrontation with Peter of which we read in chapter 8 of Mark's gospel illustrates this point. Here we find Peter who is keen to attribute every possible title and distinction to Jesus, and we find Jesus rebuking him as follows:

'Get behind me, Satan! For you are setting your mind not on divine things but on human things.' He called the crowd with his disciples, and said to them, 'If any want to become my followers, let them deny themselves and take up their cross and follow me. For those who want to save their life will lose it, and those who lose their life for my sake, and for the sake of the gospel, will save it.' (Mk 8:33b–35).

This passage makes clear that, to quote Dietrich Bonhoeffer, 'discipleship as commitment to the person of Jesus Christ puts the disciple under the law of Christ, that is under the cross'.[2] Bonhoeffer, who himself was to be crucified for Christ's sake, specifies further: 'The cross does not come with our natural existence, it comes with being a Christian.'[3] Thus, the cross of Christ forces us to make a decision. If we want to follow Jesus we are bound to suffer for his sake. To call Jesus Master, Lord, Saviour or even God, does not yet make us true followers of him. In the churches we may at times be more interested in checking other people's belief in the divinity of Jesus Christ in order to establish their orthodoxy, than in following the human Jesus to God. It is far easier to be orthodox than to follow Jesus Christ. In other words, the mere recognition of God's presence in Jesus does not yet make us Christ's followers. Our involvement in active discipleship does; but what is active discipleship?

Active discipleship is not just about shouting or singing 'Jesus, Jesus'; rather it learns from Jesus what it means to turn to this world, which God so loved that he gave his only son. Active discipleship, then, means to love and give ourselves to God so that Jesus does not remain God's only son for all eternity. We all are called to become daughters and sons of God, sisters and brothers and friends of Jesus. God loves this world so much that he accepted Jesus's own sacrifice for this world and raised him from the dead and the forgotten up to his divine presence and thus to the forefront of our memories.

Too often do we see God's raising of Jesus as an isolated event. Yet the resurrection makes sense only in the context of Jesus's whole life and ministry which eventually led him to his death on the cross. As we have seen in greater detail in the previous chapter, Jesus's resurrection can free us from all our petty worries about our individual future and its definite limitation through our death; it frees us for our response to God's call in and on behalf of his creative project here and now in this world.

4.3 Secularisation

Often we hear Christians complaining that our culture is becoming more and more secularised and that people care more and more for this world and less and less for the church. We ought to be careful not to tune too easily into the rhythm of such complaints. There is no reason for us Christians to be sad if people turn towards the world, if we ourselves wake up to our call from God and to our resulting responsibilities for God's world. There is no reason to regret that people such as Bob Geldof and the Greenpeace crews care for the world and not so much for the institution 'church', because in their genuine love for the world, for God's creatures, they too do God's will. It would be absurd to say that only denominationally organised people could do God's will. If secularisation means that we finally take up our cross and serve this world not in order to become heroes or to conquer the world for our own private purposes, but in order to serve the world in God's Spirit, that is to co-operate with God's creative activity in this world, surely then secularisation as a turn to the world must be welcomed.[4]

Secularisation in this sense means that we declare ourselves to be in active solidarity with all human beings, particularly with the needy ones, those who are hungry, those who are ill, abused and isolated, those whose lives are endangered by evil political and economical systems, those who are victims of sophisticated structures of exploitation (not only in the third world), those who are old and considered unfit to function successfully in our economies, the children whose future we are about to pollute or to destroy politically, the children who become our victims before they are even born, the women who are abused and whose full human dignity is still not accepted in many systems which continue to hail male supremacy, and of course, with all those whom we believe to be already in God's presence.

But secularisation means also that we should abandon any dualism of the sort that this world is not really real in God's view, whereas the other 'world', the supernatural realm, is really real. Secularisation means that we accept this world as willed and created by God and that we help to overcome the distortions imposed on this world by us human beings.

It is not enough to contribute our money to all those undoubtedly important collections for the poor, the needy, and for all kinds of ecological projects and concerns. God wants us to give ourselves, that we might transform the structures and occasions of evil in this world, and that we shall never cease to transform our own hearts. *Metanoiete*, turn around, cries Jesus, 'strive first for the kingdom of God and his righteousness' (Mt. 6:33). The Spirit of love guides us in this effort.

4.4. The Eucharist at the centre

Yet where do we find a common basis for all our different approaches to this search? Where do we hear again and again the call of God? Where do we find new inspiration for our response to God's call? Where do we encounter the community and the solidarity of all those who respond to God's invitation by co-operating with him in the building of his kingdom? Where do we find the space, time and language which we need in order to strengthen one another for this difficult task? Where do we find support when our own cross threatens to kill us?

From the earliest days of witness to Jesus as the risen crucified Christ, his disciples gathered around a table and celebrated the Eucharist. *Eucharistia* means thanksgiving. Yet in the Christian tradition of eucharistic celebration another dimension joined that of thanksgiving: remembrance. It is in the Eucharist that Christians have continued to find their identity again and again to this day. In spite of all the distortions which happened to the eucharistic celebration it has never lost this twofold focus of thanking God and of remembering how God revealed his plan for our salvation in the life, death and resurrection of Jesus Christ.

The Eucharist has always included the proclamation of and the listening to the good news of God's gift of new life in Christ. The readings from the Hebrew Scriptures speak of God's presence with his people Israel, of his call and their response or failure to respond. The New Testament readings speak of Jesus's ministry, death and resurrection and reflect upon his significance as Christ for us. They remind us how God has renewed his ancient call to all human beings through Jesus and how Jesus's disciples and friends have responded or failed to respond to this call.

But the Eucharist has also been a celebration. This aspect so often escapes our attention today as we all too often find ourselves in boring, empty and meaningless forms of eucharistic 'celebration'. It is therefore of vital importance that we retrieve this aspect of genuine celebration of the presence of Christ in our midst which had characterised the celebrations of the Eucharist in the early church. But even in the medieval and Tridentine church there was a sense of divine presence, a sense of the presence of the holy. It seems that in our generation we have not yet succeeded in finding our way of expressing and celebrating Christ's presence in our midst. Or is it that we no longer believe in this presence?

In order to begin to express anew this sense of Christ's presence in our community we may need to remember that the celebration of the eucharistic meal follows the example of the meal which Jesus himself ate with his friends before he was murdered. Thus, the Eucharist brings together the memory of Jesus's ministry in response to God's call on the one hand, and the interpretation by his followers of his life, death and resurrection on the other hand. The Eucharist, therefore, is the primary occasion of Christian self-understanding.

As such the Eucharist ought to be an inclusive celebration, and not an exclusive occasion in which a sectarian identity-search against others, for instance the Jewish community, is to be developed. In this context it is important to recall that the earliest church-communities were in no way separate churches against Judaism. Rather, the Christian movement started as a Jewish renewal movement, until in the aftermath of political events, such as the expulsion of the Hellenists from Jerusalem and the foundation of non-Jewish Christian communities, it developed quickly into an independent organisation. This transformation from an originally Jewish group into a universal network of communities with their own liturgical centre in the celebration of the Eucharist marks the complex beginning of what we call today the Christian church.[5]

The unity of this church, however, has always been a unity in diversity. No two churches were ever the same. Each Christian community developed under particular geographic, cultural, linguistic, political, economical and other conditions and under the influence of a particular leadership. The New Testament already gives ample evidence of the broad spectrum of Christian communities which formed themselves locally in response to God's call in Jesus Christ. Thus, the Christian tradition is in fact best understood and narrated as the story of the different Christian communities and their often different forms of connection. Yet most Christian communities celebrate the Eucharist and all of them tell the good news of God's revelation in the history of Israel and in the life, death and resurrection of Jesus Christ. This has been their common identity until today, even if the individual communities have not always been explicitly conscious of it. And this ought to be the focal point of our efforts to promote church unity today.

It is of secondary importance how we organise leadership and spiritual authority in our community (this question will be addressed in the following chapter). But it seems to me to be of primary importance for us that we all share in this eucharistic tradition. For in the Eucharist we are called again into the centre of our primary religious experience as Christians. Here we are confronted with the 'dangerous and subversive memory of Jesus Christ' (J. B. Metz) which challenges all our legalism, institutionalism, sexism, and all distortions of our faith.[6] The Eucharist reminds us anew that Jesus of Nazareth really and totally responded to God's call unto the death on the cross. We are justified in understanding this death as his self-sacrifice also for our sake, because his sacrifice allowed God to reveal his redemptive plan once and for all.

The Eucharist then frees us to relate anew to God, to one another, to God's creation, and to ourselves. The sharing of bread and wine symbolises the bond of love which reveals our true human identity and unites us all in God's Spirit. The Eucharist is thus the event in which we are re-formed both individually and communally. In the experience of the new bonding we become a proper and authentic community of God's friends. It is the occasion where we meet our true selves as accepted, forgiven and loved by God and one another. Moreover, it is here that we experience the ultimate unity of all humanity. In other words, in the Eucharist we are drawn into the mystery of God's creative project in this world.[7]

This eucharistic experience knows no limitation, no prior condition, no imposition of petty boundaries. As Jesus sat down to eat with the tax-collectors, we too are free to share our most precious experience with all people of good will who are genuinely searching for Christ's presence in our world, whatever their previous history, record of broken relationships (i.e. sins) and failure to respond to God's call. Thus the strict denominational boundaries which have emerged in the history of the Christian movement and which have split our communities until today are as such invalid. To uphold them amounts to a sinful caricature of God's free gift of love in Jesus Christ.

This is not to say that all Christian communities around the globe should be organised in one and the same way. Rather, different languages, different cultures, different political conditions call for different and creative ways of responding to God's call in Christ today in the different parts of our world. But whatever the order of a community, every Christian community is critically judged in the light of its willingness to experience Jesus Christ and of its readiness to celebrate the memory of his sacrificial love for God, for us and for this world. One criterion for assessing whether we are true followers of Christ is the way in which we celebrate the Eucharist; a second criterion is whether we reflect our eucharistic experience in our daily life.

The eucharistic character of all truly Christian communities provides the answer to our question: Church as community or as institution? The church is a dynamic network of communities of people who respond to God's call and to God's self-revelation in Jesus Christ. This understanding of church does not deny the need for particular forms of organisation of such communities. Every human community needs some form of structure and leadership. We shall discuss this aspect of the church in the next chapter. But here it is important to see that Christian communities are not true to their eucharistic character when they simply copy uncritically the structure of any given political institution or administration of some historical period or other, such as a monarchical model (following the organisational model of Constantine's Roman state) or even the institution of an absolutist state or party.

The pluralism of Christian responses, a pluralism recorded already in the New Testament, and the necessary pluralism of understanding the biblical texts in different times and cultures are not a threat to Christian identity. Rather this essential pluralism provides the challenge for the different Christian communities in the world to build their community wherever they are, while contributing at the same time to the co-operation and solidarity of the global network of all Christian communities in the world. To think of the kingdom of God only in black and white terms, i.e. which *form* of response is right and which is wrong, would cause a serious breakdown of human appreciation of the beautiful variety found in God's creation.

For instance, any effort to impose a basically Graeco-Roman concept of church structure combined with a

nineteenth- or twentieth-century model of European
nationalism on the whole set of Christian communities in
this world would be just another way of displaying
cultural imperialism and limiting the creative inclusive-
ness of our eucharistic self-understanding. Christians in
every part of the world must attempt to find their own
eucharistic way in response to God's call in Christ and
refrain from imposing their particular way of responding
on other communities in different parts of the world. To
think that God would look only for one conformist
response to his call means to misunderstand God's
creative project as it has become revealed in the
Scriptures and traditions of the Christian movement.

4.5. The Eucharist as a criterion for church reform

Where then is the true church today? It is indeed
everywhere where people genuinely attempt to respond
to God's call and help to build God's world. We
experience ourselves as free creatures, free to say 'Yes' or
'No' to God's call. We are free to accept the Spirit of Jesus
Christ as our guide. We are free to allow ourselves to be
confronted by God's love and its consequences for us in
the celebration of the Eucharist. And we are free to trust
in Jesus's promise that wherever two or three are
gathered in his name, there his Spirit will unfold God's
own dynamics (Mt. 18:20).

The Eucharist is, of course, not the only occasion of
proclaiming, celebrating, and sharing the new life in
Christ. There are countless ways in which Christians can
respond to God's call. But the Eucharist is the most
intensified, the most dense, the most complex
sacramental expression and experience of Christian life in
God's presence. It unites all experiences of God's

presence in one single celebration, and, at the same time, it allows us to commit ourselves as a community of disciples to God's great creative project. Thus, the Eucharist is neither the only experience of our call, nor the only expression of our response to God's call in Christ. Rather, the Eucharist anticipates the fullness of life with God, and therefore it invites all expressions of authentic Christian life to join into its never-ending feast of renewal of life beyond all forms of death. The Eucharist will therefore always form the centre of Christian existence and provide us with an important criterion as to how serious we are about living this new life beyond death ('eternal life') already here and now.

The ecumenical movement in this century has correctly highlighted the importance for the Christian churches of working together towards a mutual recognition of the different Christian ways of celebrating the Eucharist. In this context the question of intercommunion, that is the full participation of Christians from different denominations in each other's eucharistic celebrations, has been raised. Some Christian church leaders have expressed the view that intercommunion should be the ultimate goal of ecumenical rapprochement, others advocate the extension of an immediate eucharistic hospitality to their fellow Christians from other denominations. At the moment there is some confusion about this point in the Christian movement.

From the theological perspective which underlines my treatment of the Eucharist in this chapter, I cannot but side with those who already now recognise the different eucharistic celebrations throughout Christianity as occasions where the new life in Christ is proclaimed, celebrated and really shared. Thus, intercommunion is for me not a goal for the church of the future, but a means to experience more of the kingdom of God now. No church has a right to own its own eucharistic celebration in the name of some church rule or law. Rather, the Eucharist is the occasion where the coming kingdom of God becomes so real that denominational boundaries are automatically transcended by the experience of Christ's presence. Jesus Christ is the host of the eucharistic feast, not any particular church or denomination. Hence the inclusive nature of the genuine eucharistic experience cannot be emphasised enough in the current debates on who should be invited to what Eucharist.

However, the richness of our eucharistic heritage is not always adequately reflected in the spiritual and liturgical life of Christian communities.

4.6 Liturgy and eucharistic spirituality

Liturgical expressions are among the most influential manifestations of the communal character of our Christian faith. In our liturgical gatherings we attempt to retrieve the centre of our faith in word and action, and we try to make it contemporaneous. That means we try to appropriate the foundational experiences of our faith in the space, time and language of our own world. This appropriation can, of course, only be successful if we have some understanding of the resources of our faith and also of the world in which we are trying to live this faith. Hence any adequate liturgy includes both a proper recollection of the sources of our faith and a strategic reflection on how to practise this faith in the present time. Any such strategic reflection must, however, be open to the element of surprise. If our liturgies are planned to such an extent that no surprising insight into God's mysterious presence in

Christ can occur, they have failed in their very purpose of renewing our relationship with God.

What I have said so far must not be misunderstood as an over-intellectual definition of Christian liturgy. Rather it is an attempt to discuss in theological terms what liturgical action entails. But any liturgical action is always more than conscious and self-conscious reflection, it is first of all a symbolic activity.

A symbol is a very precious means of communication. It always unites an ordinary experience of our life with a special interpretation. In baptism, for instance, we use the ordinary experience of washing our bodies and load it with the special meaning of cleansing our entire relational capacity. As we clean our bodies in the ordinary act of washing, so we clean our entire human being in the ritual of baptism. The symbolic action of baptism draws us into a new way of relating to God, each other, God's creation and ourselves. Thus, it would be foolish to think that baptism was 'only a symbol'. Rather we should learn to appreciate that a symbol is one of the richest ways of expressing and communicating our divine–human and inter-human relationships.

Unlike baptism, the eucharistic celebration involves us in a frequently repeated symbolic activity. In most Christian churches baptism is a unique event in our life, mostly occurring in our childhood before we have reached a sufficient level of consciousness either to actively participate in the symbolic action or to remember this experience later on in life. But the Eucharist involves us on every level of our personality.

In the liturgy of the Eucharist we are both mentally and physically drawn into the mystery of God's presence in Christ and into the mystery of the living body of Christ,

i.e. the Christian community. The traditional debates on
how to express best this divine presence have at times
overshadowed the actual experience of this presence. In
the old medieval way of expressing the understanding of
divine presence, reference was made to 'supernature'
breaking into our ordinary 'nature'. The language of the
transubstantiation of bread and wine was one attempt to
grasp that new breaking in of God's realm into our
human realm.

Nowadays we have a different understanding of
'nature'; we appreciate all nature as God's creation,
although we often do not relate to it as God wishes us to.
But the awareness of our sinfulness should never lead us
to downgrade God's creative project here and now.
Therefore, I think that it is more adequate to talk of one
nature rather than of nature and supernature. However, it
is crucial to understand God's offer of presence here and
now. And it is this healing and transforming presence
which we proclaim, celebrate and share in the Eucharist.
This threefold experience is not only mental, but also
physical. Our entire humanity is drawn into God's
presence in Christ during the eucharistic liturgy. What
more could God give us than this wonderful experience
of his creative and redemptive presence? Our entire life,
all of our relationships, our concrete experience of a
community responding to God's call in Christ, everything
is to be transformed in this symbolic action. The Greek
verb *symbolein* means 'to throw together'. Everything is
brought together in the Eucharist and thus can be
changed. In the Eucharist we gain an experience of the
whole. Here we can taste and feel eternal life.
Unfortunately, our concrete eucharistic experience may
not always be of the sort just described.

With regard to our liturgical praxis in general my thesis is that our liturgies can only be as good as our faith is at the time. We cannot hope to be renewed and transformed by our liturgies if our faith is not open to some form of rediscovery, transformation and surprise. If our faith does not expect anything from God and from ourselves, we cannot expect anything from our liturgical action either. In other words, if we are not prepared to see anew how God wishes us to relate to him, to each other, to his world, and to ourselves, we will not see anything new. However, if we truly wish to see and experience our faith anew in our liturgical gatherings, then we may find a deeper appreciation of God's call in Christ and of the emerging kingdom of God.

There is then a dialectical relationship between liturgy and faith. An adventurous faith will tend to organise more adventurous forms of liturgy. A boring faith will prefer boring liturgies. To complain about the state of our liturgies in our church, yet at the same time not to complain about the state of our faith, is schizophrenic. In other words, we can only hope to renew our liturgical praxis once we are prepared to renew both our faith in God's call and our willingness to respond to this call in this world.

The following questions come to mind in this context: Do our liturgies mirror the God-given freedom of a Christian community gathered in the name of Jesus Christ? Are our liturgies open to God's surprising presence in our midst or are our liturgies organised with the aim of keeping God's surprising presence at bay? Do our liturgies reflect the radical equality of God's kingdom? Are our liturgies occasions of joy, hope and expectation? Are they hallmarks of transformation of both our life as

Christian community and of our action in and for this world? Formulated in one sentence: Do our liturgies advance the arrival of God's kingdom?

Our criteria for assessing the church's overall relationship to God's kingdom must be applied here as well. We must review our liturgies in terms of how they could help us to know more about God's loving presence, more about God's call, more about our possibilities of responding to this call. Do our liturgies help us to advance our experience of the freedom to love, the equality to serve, and our readiness to be surprised by God?

Let us return to the liturgy of the Eucharist. Does our eucharistic experience really help women, men and children in the pews to develop a sense, a taste of the freedom of God's kingdom? Does the clergy–laity divide present in the eucharistic celebration of some churches enhance our appreciation that we are all equally responsible for God's kingdom? What has gone wrong with our eucharistic celebration?

Without going into great historical detail here it may be of importance for us to understand some of our present problems with the Eucharist from an historical perspective.[8] Since the Middle Ages the sacrificial aspect of the Eucharist has been overemphasised to the detriment of the communal aspect. What I mean here is the belief that the re-enactment of Christ's sacrificial death provides the atonement for our sins, and that this re-enactment could only be undertaken by a person who has been empowered to act *in persona Christi*. This overconcentration on the removal of individual guilt and the underemphasis on the communal responsibility to co-create this universe with God has led both to the acknowledgment of the special mediatory power of the priest and to the general passivity of the Mass goers. To have been there, has often been more significant for the ordinary Christian than to participate actively in the eucharistic celebration itself. To have been in touch with the sacred sacrifice has often been considered the main aim of the Christian. And at a time when the church was in fact identified with God's kingdom on earth this experience of being in touch with the sacred centre could naturally be perceived as a rewarding event.

Today, however, we see the difference between the church and God's kingdom more clearly. We know that we are not the sole producers of God's reign; we are only co-producers. But that we are, and this dignity gives all of us disciples of Christ a much greater task than just to be in touch with the sacred sacrifice, and also a greater task than just to hope for the forgiveness of our individual sins. As we have seen above, God's kingdom is about the transformation of all of our relationships.

In order to avoid any possible misunderstanding, both to be in touch with the sacred centre of our life and to experience God's forgiveness for our 'No' to his call are important aspects of our eucharistic celebration. But our Eucharist is more: it is also the celebration of God's presence in all the spheres of our existence: biological, spiritual, economic, social, political, aesthetic etc. Every aspect of our universe is sacred, graced by God's creative and redemptive presence. Jesus Christ's ministry, death and resurrection have freed us to grasp anew the proper relationship between God and his creation, and the proper approach to God's mystery. God is not a distant patriarch who allows us occasionally to get in touch with him through the special mediation of sacred men or women.

Rather God is proclaimed as the loving parent who is close to all of us at all times and everywhere. He[9] loves his creatures and his creative project and he is deeply concerned about our frequent refusal to respond to his call on us to become active fellow builders of his reign.

The Eucharist is that sacrament which reminds us best that our entire existence in God's presence is sacramental. The Eucharist must therefore not be reduced either to a mere intellectual discourse with perhaps some music here and there as in some reformed traditions, nor to a totally formalised symbolic action whose meaning is no longer understood by us today, as is often the case in Anglican and Roman Catholic churches. We do need symbolic action, but we also need to understand its purpose and its form in order to participate actively in it. Yet we also need to participate in it in order to understand it. Therefore I think that an important task for liturgists must be to redress the balance in the eucharistic celebration between intellectual participation on the one hand and physical and emotional participation on the other. Once both aspects are better co-ordinated we may begin to prepare more adequately for our eucharistic gatherings. Thus the improvement of our Eucharist depends not only on our willingness to participate in it, but also on our renewed understanding of what it actually is, in what we are supposed to participate, when the community gathers for its foundational celebration.

4.7 Conclusion

Too often nowadays the Eucharist is discussed in terms of who should celebrate it on whose behalf. Questions of male or female clergy, of church order and ontological requirements for priests have overshadowed the perception of what the Eucharist means for Christian life. Therefore it seemed to me appropriate to disentangle the question of church structure from the discussion of the centrality of eucharistic celebration in the church. However, as we saw already, we never celebrate anything in a vacuum. Rather our cultural identity co-determines our celebration of the Eucharist. Our concepts of leadership influence our ways of organising our celebrations and the whole of our Christian existence. We therefore must attend now to the question of leadership, ministry and authority in the church. But this discussion is a function of our primary experience of God's love, presence and call in Christ, and never vice versa.

5

LEADERSHIP AND AUTHORITY

5.0 Introduction

In this chapter I would like to examine the nature of
Christian ministry and the need for leadership in the
Christian community. Any consideration of adequate
structures of organising our response to God's call in
Christ is, of course, dependent on our understanding of
that call. Hence, our reflection on the institutional
organisation of Christian community is dependent on our
continuous reflection on God's call. Any replacement of
wrong or obsolete structures in our churches will spring
from our openness to explore again and again, with
critical and self-critical eyes, the resources of our Christian
faith in God.

5.1 The crisis of authority in church and society

There is a broad consensus that at present the Christian
church is experiencing a crisis of authority. This crisis
takes different forms in different churches. While many
Roman Catholics struggle with the monarchical and
hierarchical constitution of their church, many Protestant
Christians despair over the absence of any clearly defined
central leadership. Thus, Christians today can suffer from
an absence of leadership as well as from an overdose of
leadership.

Although the reactions to this crisis of authority and
leadership in the church vary significantly, the diagnosis
of the fact of this crisis is widely shared. Of course, this

experience of a crisis of authority is not unique to the Christian church. The phenomenon is acutely felt in all realms of our Western cultures: parental authority, educational authority, spiritual authority, political authority, military authority and many other forms of authority have become objects of great suspicion. Whose interests do these forms of authority represent? Does authority only wish to maintain a certain order suitable to those who already hold power, or should authority be handled in such a way as to promote the greatest possible emancipation of and participation by individual people in the common good?

In this situation of confusion about authority in our cultures, many commentators have strongly urged that we ought to relocate ourselves in the best of our classical traditions of knowing and acting. The Greek heritage, the biblical and post-biblical Christian traditions, revised forms of communism and other models from the past have been recommended by some commentators for a constructive retrieval today, while other analysts have warned against any such effort of looking for orientation and authority solely in the past. Similarly, the theological debate in the Christian churches has reached the point where some theologians see salvation from our current crisis of authority only in models established by certain epochs of Christian history (e.g. first-century Christian life; nineteenth-century integralism, etc.), while others continue to warn against any uncritical acceptance of any particular leadership model of our past.

It is essential then for Christians to reflect again on the foundations of authority in any Christian community. As has become clear already in the first chapter of this book, the Christian community owes all of its authority to God and not to itself. God is the sole *auctor* of the community. God has called his people into a religious, social, political, linguistic, cultural, geographic and economical existence by inviting men, women and children to respond together to his presence in this universe. Recognising God's ultimate and superior authority, the community is fundamentally suspicious of all human claims to ultimate authority and to superiority. Thus with regard to the forms of their organisation we can say that the members of a Christian community, by nature of their call should act in an 'anti-authoritarian' manner towards each other.

'Anti-authoritarian' refers to the need to question again and again the legitimacy of the forms of authority employed in the churches, but it does not mean that there should not be such forms at all. A Christian community, like any other human community, needs some structures and clearly designed social functions in order to minimise potential conflicts and tensions. However, Christian communities must be particularly mindful that no such function or structure develop into a system of oppression where spiritually legitimised authority is replaced by spiritually unjustifiable exercise of power by one section of the community over the other.

5.2 Authority in the Christian community in historical perspective

From a sociological perspective, 'the phenomenon of authority is basic to human behaviour'.[1] Authority can be defined as a property of a person or office, a relationship, a quality of communication or as a variation of one or more of these; it can be observed as parental authority (family), leadership in groups, as organised and bureaucratic authority (schools, churches, armies, industrial and governmental agencies, etc.), and generally as political authority. With regard to 'authority' we have to analyse now whether or not the social reality of the Christian church has been reflecting the spiritual identity of the Christian community as we have understood it in this book.

The history of the Christian church illustrates the fact that different forms of authority have always existed in the church and that there has always been a conflict about what constitutes 'authentic' authority in the community of Christians. In the early church, for instance, the homeless wandering charismatics played an important role.[2] Much more than any local group of Christians they represented 'authoritatively' the new faith-praxis (cf. Paul and Barnabas). The authority of these wandering charismatics was recognised and affirmed by the local communities as superior to their own emerging leadership. However, the tension between the prophetic element and the more conservative forces within the local communities can be observed already very early in the Christian movement.[3] As the stabilisation of the local communities progressed, models for their organisation were taken at first from Jewish and other contemporary religious traditions (cultic offices and officers), and then, after the Constantinian changes in the fourth century, increasingly from the praxis of political and legal organisation in the Roman and subsequent secular empires. This latter source explains to some extent such organisational trends as the development of the territorial principle in parish structures, the growing distinction between clergy and laity, and the progressing centralisation within the church, such as the primacy of

Rome which began to emerge from the end of the second century onwards.

This way of organising Christian community was not accepted by all members of the community, as the development of monastic forms of Christian life illustrates. Various monastic communities tried to preserve some of the egalitarian and prophetic identity of the Christian community. Yet even these more adventurous forms of Christian community were in constant danger of being 'co-ordinated' by Roman or local bishops on the one hand and by local or imperial politicians on the other.

Structurally, the medieval church consisted of two essentially ('ontologically') different sections, the clergy and the laity.[4] The clergy had become the ruling class while the laity was the group to be looked after (not always only spiritually) by the clergy. This ecclesiastical organisation was questioned in the Protestant Reformation which retrieved the biblical image of the priesthood of all believers. But this retrieval was at first more of a programmatic nature, while the actual situation in the local church remained largely unchanged. The Protestant 'pastor' continued to take care of his flock, the Protestant potentate took over the role of the civil patron of the Reformed Church from his Roman Catholic predecessor. However, the ecclesial reorganisation in many (though not in all) Protestant movements led eventually to a much more substantial participation of the 'laity' in church government, whereas in the Roman Catholic Church the principle of clerical authority was refined even further. Here the clerical absolutism has on the whole remained unchanged until today.

While many Protestant churches consider the offices in

the church as functions whose authority springs from the community, the Roman Catholic Church continues to defend the status of its male clergy as willed by Christ. Thus, the organisation of authority in this church is seen to come directly from God and to demand absolute obedience from the members of the community. The model of vicarious representation of authority in the Roman Church has survived even the changes of the Second Vatican Council. Although the Council's Constitution on the Church (*Lumen Gentium*) describes the church as the people of God and emphasises the equal importance of all its members,[5] the equality of the faithful breaks down when in the same document we 'do not meet the view of one priestly character and diversity of function but two ontological qualities, resulting in two essentially different lines of functions, whereof the one is representative and the other is not'.[6] The tragedy of the Second Vatican Council lies in its failure to agree wholeheartedly on the redefinition of the church as community and to abandon the concept of the church as *societas* [society]. As long as the final power over the community remains only in the hands of one section of the community, the essence of community authorised by God is destroyed in favour of an ecclesial society authorised only by itself.

Nevertheless, the ambiguity of *Lumen Gentium* and the spirit of the Constitution *Gaudium et Spes* have been interpreted by some sections of the Roman Catholic Church as invitations to work for a more authentic communal faith-praxis with appropriate structures. The Latin American base-communities are one important example of this renewal in spite of the continuing authoritarian government of the Roman Catholic Church.

Since the beginning of the modern period, particularly as a result of the Enlightenment, all the Christian churches have been confronted with a radical critique of all forms of authority which cannot be accounted for by intelligible and persuasive arguments. Hence all the churches are called to defend publicly all aspects of their organisational structure. Yet the leadership of the Roman Catholic Church in particular has failed to meet this critique from within and from outside the church, and it continues to assert its status mainly by operating a system of appointing and controlling bishops and theologians.[7]

Three responses to this situation can be observed within today's Roman Catholic Church: (1) An affirmative attitude towards this system found among obedient lay-people who favour the shepherd-flock model of church authority over against the organisation of a community in which every member shares the same rights and duties. Ironically, the shepherd-flock model of church organisa-tion is supported vigorously by powerful movements within this Church, such as Opus Dei, who claim to be mainly lay organisations. (2) A twofold response among critical lay-people who would like to help to build a local community with or without clerical leadership while at the same time trying to promote change in the system of church government. (3) A radical departure from all Roman Catholic and similar forms of clerical absolutism in favour of alternative models of a church characterised by principally 'non-institutional' forms of Christian com-munities, so-called 'house churches', fellowships, etc.

While all Protestant churches embrace in principle at least the priesthood of all believers, they too face a crisis of authority. Does the ultimate authority in Christian faith rest with the individual believer alone or is the community of Christians the proper source of Christian authority? As one Presbyterian pastor once remarked to me, in the Roman Catholic Church they would have to endure only one pope, whereas he faced seven at every presbytery meeting.

In this situation of conflict and crisis, it must be the task of the theologian to reflect anew upon the spiritual foundation of Christian community and upon the dimensions of authority within the community, and to offer both a critique of existing forms of authority and proposals for a better organisation of church. Any reflection on the organisation of Christian community will have to consider at least three aspects of the church: its institutional character, its organisation of leadership and service, and its openness to critique and reform.

5.3 The institutional character of the church

The problem for Christians is not that they have organised themselves in ways which allow for stable and lasting communities and an uninterrupted tradition of response to God's call, but the question is: Which forms of institution are more equipped to promote Christian faith-praxis and which are less, not at all, or no longer suitable?

As we have already seen, Christian communities have often adopted models for their own social organisation from the political context in which the communities developed. One of the reasons for this choice was the platonic understanding of Christian community as perfect society, that is the perfect earthly reflection of the divine essence of church. As society, the church favoured institutional means by which it could rapidly accelerate its development all over the world, that is to achieve the highest possible realisation of its divine essence. This aim brought it into conflict with the secular powers interested in ruling the same world, so that the conflict between 'throne' and 'altar' arose. In this situation the leadership of the church has at times given in to the temptation to understand the church as a political power and often even as a military body in this world.

As a result of the radical cultural, political and theological changes in modern times, the image of the church as perfect society has been widely discredited in favour of a more biblically inspired image, namely the church as community. This image describes a community which is no longer interested in conquering the globe in military terms, but which tries to witness as best it can to its foundational experiences of God's call in a more and more secularised world. This new self-understanding of the church based on personal and communal experience rather than on metaphysical deduction calls for a diversity of organisational models in order to fulfil its mission in a pluralistic world.

The spiritual vocation of Christian communities and their necessarily pluralistic response call for forms of institution which are open to being adapted to the particular needs of the local community rather than institutions which try to determine the response to God's call in the local community from outside. The vocation of the Christian community implies then a rejection of all authoritarian forms of institution. Moreover this exper-iential nature of Christian faith and the belief that God alone has authority over the community unite in a forceful rejection of all forms of *absolute* human authority.

In order to preserve the freedom of the individual in the church on the one hand, and the spiritual dignity of the Christian community on the other, it has been suggested above (1.5) that the church be organised as an 'institutional an-archy'. Such an understanding of Christian community could promote the actual sharing of power and responsibility as well as the unmasking of all misuses of power in the church. The need for a continuous transformation of the institutional dimensions of the church arises from the changing perception of what constitutes an adequate response to the gospel in our time and its different contexts. 'No community can exist without some institutionalisation that lends it unity, coherency, and identity. The institution does not exist for itself but is in service to the community of faith. As such, it evolves, following the same path as the historical transformation of the community itself that faces crises and discovers institutional responses to them. What we call ongoing conversion belongs to this historical process of fidelity and service to the community and the Lord.'[8] But it is important that this need for conversion is not limited to the individual believer. 'If conversion does not reach the institution of the Church, if it does not call into question the way in which power is exercised, if it does not reach the wider society, then we cannot speak of gospel conversion.'[9] The criterion of our religious institutions must remain the gospel.

Of course, the gospel must be interpreted anew in every generation and context. Such interpretation will always be pluralistic by nature of the different perspectives and contexts of the interpreters. This pluralism is not only no threat to the gospel; rather it alerts the community to realise its particular limitations and, thus, to look out to other Christian communities, past and present, for critical correctives and encouragement.[10]

This understanding of the need for and the limitations of institutional dimensions in the church has direct consequences for our understanding of authentic leadership in the Christian community.

5.4 Leadership and ministry in the church

Leadership is a function of the Christian community and not a status over against it.[11] The abolition of class structures in the church (laity and clergy) and the integration of all the different gifts (*charismata*) of the Spirit in the community are preconditions for a church trying to respond faithfully to the particular religious and social initiatives of Jesus Christ and his disciples. While the diversity of gifts in the community must be seen as a blessing, the organisation of these gifts for the benefit of the community's faith-praxis may give rise to conflict. However, the crucial point is not that there may be disagreement and diversity of opinions in the community as to how to organise itself; rather the essential question is how to handle such conflict and diversity in faithfulness to Christ's uniting and constructive Spirit. Fortunately, the Christian tradition offers not only negative examples but also promising ways of handling conflict within the community for the benefit of the entire church. For instance, Peter, James and Paul reached an understanding in their debate on who should be allowed to become a member of the church, only Jews and circumcised Gentiles, or everybody who believes in Jesus Christ (Galatians 2 and Acts 15).

As already mentioned above (1.4) the ongoing discussion in the Christian churches about equality between men and women in terms of access to the ordained ministry, as important as it is for a more adequate appreciation of the role of women in the Christian community, may at times have also a distorting effect on the general discussion of the nature of ministry. The particular focus on women has overshadowed the more general need for a radical reassessment of the nature of authentic Christian faith-praxis and its implications for appropriate organisation of Christian leadership and the different ministries in the Christian communities.

Only in the framework of a fundamental debate on the question of what constitutes authentic Christian faith can we reconsider the specific issue of the ordained ministry. That a human community requires some form of leadership is beyond doubt. That the Christian community needs an ordained ministry, however, cannot be taken for granted,[12] but needs to be discussed with reference to both the spiritual and institutional demands of a contemporary human association. In view of these requirements it seems rather odd that in some Christian churches the particular understanding of the ordained ministry is still largely focused on by now obsolete metaphysical categories of personal transformation at the point of ordination and on the organisational needs of medieval congregations.

Most urgently needed is a reassessment of the relationship between the ordained minister and the ordaining community. The two-class system which developed particularly in the Anglican Church and the Roman Catholic Church with their practice of 'absolute' ordinations of priests and bishops, i.e. the ordination of men (and women) without any connection to a particular community, and – in the Roman Catholic Church – the imposition of 'leaders' on communities or entire dioceses without their consent, cannot be justified either by reference to the New Testament or by any other intelligible spiritual and theological criteria.

Of course, there may be emergencies where a community is unable or unwilling to ordain or appoint its own minister and therefore needs the support of other Christian communities, or where a community as a whole is engaged in a praxis which other communities regard as no longer Christian, that is as no longer responding to God's call in Jesus Christ. In such extraordinary situations it may well be necessary for fellow communities to become active and try to help out by making a more responsible leadership available for a particular period in time. But such emergencies must not be cited in order to justify the current praxis of absolute ordination and appointment which deprives many Christian congregations and dioceses of their basic dignity as Christian communities.

The argument most often quoted in favour of the Roman Catholic organisation of a centrally managed leadership, i.e. the hierarchy of officers: pope, bishops, priests, is the need to preserve the apostolic tradition in the Christian church. Some other churches are equally intent on preserving that tradition though they do not perceive the need for a global patriarch. However, the apostolic tradition might be preserved equally well if not better through an organisation of Christian community where each member shares in the joy of witnessing to the presence of Christ's Spirit in their midst by being actively engaged in the threefold praxis of the community described above (2.5.1), namely to proclaim, celebrate and share the new life in Jesus Christ. Centralism as a principle of organisation does not guarantee the integrity of our response to God's call any better than a truly community-based form of organisation of our response. In fact it may well be that the latter will bring local communities to a new life, as can be witnessed already in South America, South Africa, and elsewhere, where Christian communities have successfully retrieved their own spiritual and organisational dignity.

5.5 Prophetic critique in the church

The recognition of God's authority in the church is in itself a powerful corrective to all possible misuses of authority and power in the Christian community. However, as the Roman Catholic interpretation of the vicarious foundation of church authority and power and its hierarchical results have demonstrated, appeals to God's authority can be easily misunderstood and misused in a way which divides a community into two or more classes of response to God's call instead of uniting it. Therefore Karl Rahner was correct to warn against all too quick references to God's authority in order to sanction or challenge particular expressions of human authority and power. He reminded us that our understanding of God's authority arises always from human experience. Thus, we must be critical of the distortions already present in our most basic sets of religious experiences. The authority of God is then the goal which we are to recognise better and better rather than a foundation for invoking God to support all sorts of causes.[13]

Moreover, as various developments of an uncritical self-righteousness in many Christian churches have shown, the faith-praxis of entire communities may in fact be distorted at a time. Thus, the recognition of the authority of the community and its spiritual foundation is not yet a guarantee against failure in the church. The mere profession of faith in the guidance of the Holy Spirit does not yet protect us from more subtle forms of self-deception. Therefore, we have to acknowledge the critical dimension of that same Spirit and the transformation of our faith-praxis it calls for.

The Spirit of God is the Spirit of truth. When we give up asking the question of truth we are in immediate danger of becoming self-righteous and distorted in our faith-praxis. When we no longer ask whether or not our traditional response to God's call is true, we have surrendered to our own story or journey. Of course, we are not able ultimately to judge whether our community's attempt to respond to God is true or not, but by at least asking the question we admit already in principle the fallibility of our response to God's call and may thus become open to self-critique.

In the Jewish and Christian tradition it has always been the vocation of charismatic figures, such as the prophets, to interrupt the ongoing story by asking if it was true, if it corresponded to God's will. Individual Christians as well as entire local communities can become prophetic in this sense and serve the universal church by calling it back to obedience to God's authority.

The church needs these three elements of authority: a communal organisation, an elected leadership, and the ongoing prophetic critique of both. As soon as one of these elements is missing, the faith-praxis of the community is in danger of being distorted. The way in which a Christian community and its leadership treat criticism of their particular praxis will always be an indication of their inclination towards developing either into a more loving community or a more powerful society. The church needs the continuous reflection upon its spiritual identity and a continuous critique of all kinds of ideological distortions of this identity.

5.6 Local and universal church

The existing plurality of Christian churches and the ecumenical conversation in which most of them are involved have promoted an increasing awareness of the different possibilities of organising Christian communities. The retrieval of the plurality of church responses to the gospel in New Testament times has further encouraged the appreciation of the fact that such a plurality in no way constitutes a threat to Christian faith. Rather it is a consequence of the many different contexts in which Christians have been responding to God's call. These insights have worked to highlight the need for a more detailed study of the relationship between faith and culture and of the status of the local community within the global church.[14]

In this regard the work by Robert Schreiter on *Constructing Local Theologies* is very helpful. Schreiter points out that the Christian tradition is in fact nothing other than 'a series of local theologies, closely wedded to and responding to different cultural conditions'.[15] The consequence of this shift in perspective is that no particular local theology can claim any longer to represent the whole of the Christian tradition. Rather, the Christian tradition consists of all authentic Christian communities past and present with their particular traditions. The crucial question arising from such a description of church reality then concerns the set of criteria by which to judge the authenticity of any particular local community, or in other words, the criteria for Christian identity.

However, even these criteria must be developed in a co-operative way by the various communities, rather than imposed by one community on the whole of the church. All Christian communities are called by the gospel to proclaim, to celebrate and to share the new life in Christ in their particular local situation. If they take this call seriously they will have to become as aware as possible of the situation in which they live and of the particular cultural necessities for an adequate local response to the gospel. This process of the inculturation of the gospel is never free of dangers. The local church is, by nature of its particularity, in danger of losing sight of important dimensions of the Christian faith. It needs the co-operation and constructive critique of other Christian communities. While such a co-operation is in itself never an insurance against inauthenticity, it may at least contribute to keeping alive the consciousness of possible failure and distortion in any local appropriation of the Christian faith.[16] Since there is no blueprint for criteria of authenticity, the critical and self-critical participation of every Christian community in this universal and continuous reflection on the truthfulness of Christian responses to the gospel is essential.

This universal and mutually critical co-operation among Christian communities is the context in which we ought to consider the ecumenical movement in Christianity. Without disrespect for the progress achieved so far through ecumenical dialogue, the principles, aims and agendas of this dialogue call for some critical observations.

First of all, the authority of the dialogue partners varies enormously. According to the particular constitution and self-understanding of networks of local communities, delegates are either appointed by a leadership body in the name and with the consent of the community or, as in the case of the Roman Catholic Church, by a self-appointed body of bishops without proper consultation of the community. Similarly, proposals by ecumenical committees are either accepted by the church comm-unities or only by its leadership. That is one of the most severe drawbacks of the present ecumenical process, that committees are at work often without the full participation of the communities involved, so that the ecumenical committees can unfold their own dynamics quite apart from the people for whom they claim to work. The result of this situation is that sophisticated formulas worked out by such committees have no direct bearing on any of the local communities, while at the same time, the co-operation between church traditions has progressed much more on the local level than the appropriate committees might realise and reflect.

The aim of the ecumenical movement has been to bring the different Christian churches closer together on the way towards a full Christian unity. However, over the years the perception of 'unity' has changed. In the light of the contemporary analysis of the complex relationship between faith and culture, Christian unity can certainly no longer mean a total doctrinal, liturgical and organisational uniformity or standardisation.

Standardisation and uniformity were hallmarks of a eurocentric church ever since the time of the Crusades. As long as Christian faith and European culture were exported as one single package, Christianity served more to destroy other cultures than to allow people in other cultures to develop their own social, linguistic, liturgical, theological, philosophical and artistic forms of authentic response to God's call in Jesus Christ.

Christian unity today, therefore, ought to aim at fostering the mutually critical recognition of necessarily other, though not incompatible, forms of Christian discipleship in different contexts. The ecumenical movement could thus urge the different Christian communities within one tradition as well as the different traditions to declare and practise such a unity, a true 'catholicity', rather than to limit its attention to theological and ecclesiastical diplomacy. In this context it is crucial to appreciate that Christian unity is not at the discretion of a (sometimes self-appointed) clerical leadership, but it emerges and comes to life when local communities begin to respond in a co-operative, responsible and mutually critical way to God's universal call in Jesus Christ.

Primary expressions of this catholicity of Christian faith-praxis could among other activities be intercommunion, that is the invited participation in another community's eucharistic celebration, and intercommunal solidarity and concern for the transformation of this world (see also above 4.5).[17]

5.7 Participating in God's future

Our discussion of the authority of the Christian community started with the recognition that the response called for by God's call in Jesus Christ is necessarily communal and contextual. In a particular situation, a particular time, a particular language, a particular culture we proclaim, celebrate and share God's new life as we see it disclosed in the story of Jesus Christ's ministry, death and resurrection, in God's creation and in the history of the Christian movement. Faithfulness to this disclosure rules out any reduction of our response to an exclusively private and individualistic praxis on the one hand and to any over-centralisation and over-standardisation of the various dimensions of our responses on the other hand. The first would limit the impact of Christian faith on the world, the second would hinder the appropriation of Christian faith in a given context and thus ultimately lead to the destruction of this faith's creativity in proclaiming and living the gospel in different contexts.

However, the theological and organisational insights into the communitarian character of the Christian faith-praxis do not yet free this praxis from possible distortions. Fear, the search for security, personal ambition, clerical careerism, misguided efforts of conserving the ecclesial status quo of a particular age, the lack of self-criticism in terms of appreciating the particularity of any appropriation of faith, and the temptation to prescribe one way of responding to God's call as the only possible one for all times: these and other dangers will always need to be recognised and met with critical eyes and repenting hearts. No one Christian community lives outside the conditions of this universe, and thus, every community lives in the tension between the 'already' of God's call and promise of presence and the 'not yet' of its own response (cf. above 4.1).

We understand God's call in Jesus Christ as a call to accept God's new life and thus to overcome the many manifestations of death in our world. However, if any Christian community wishes truly to respond to God's call, it will have to detect and overcome first of all the manifestations of death in its own midst. To remain or to become *ecclesia semper reformanda* (a church always to be reformed) is not a pious wish but a costly programme for every Christian community. The community's institutional presence, its leadership, and its commitment to prophetic critique and self-critique need to be examined continuously if distortions are to be detected. Hence, no claim to authority must be accepted unquestioned. Instead any such claim must be assessed by the community in terms of its faithfulness to the gospel and its service to the community.

If the Christian communities wish to respond faithfully to God's call at the end of the twentieth century, then they must be free to meet the present world in which they live, and critically but co-operatively share the common concern of all people of good will for the future of this universe. With the dismantling of the eurocentric ideologies of 'true' Christianity, new and exciting possibilities of appropriating the gospel may appear and call for critical assessment.[18] The fact that every new inculturation of the gospel may entail a possible loss of the gospel's identity should not impel us to develop neurotic measures of 'saving' our Christian identity by glorifying certain models of church from the past, such as Tridentine and post-Reformation orthodoxies. 'Orthodoxy' (that is the right teaching) and 'ortho-praxis' (that is the right way of living) cannot be defined once and for all. Rather they have to be determined again and again by each of the Christian communities and by all of them together.

The church as the universal network of all Christian communities represents nothing other than the human and fallible response to God's creative and salvific activity in this universe. Hence, the Christian community's concern for the future of this universe does not imply a loss of church identity, rather the church finds its dynamic identity only in its critical relation to the world. In this sense, the Christian community must continue to develop a spirituality of the world.[19]

The eschatological openness to God's ultimate transformation of this universe forces the church to abandon all totalitarian explanations of and approaches to the world. Instead it is the task of the church to proclaim to the world that God has invited every man, woman and child to join the process of transforming this universe according to God's creative plan. Because God has invited everyone, any lack of respect for the spiritual authority of any individual human being and of any particular community within the Christian movement would mean a failure to respect the full diversity of gifts present in the church. Equally, any refusal to co-operate and the total or partial withdrawal from such participation in God's creative project by individual Christians and by Christian communities would limit the church's response to God's call.

Even the often only too understandable frustration of individual Christians and of entire communities within the church caused by the lack of 'progress' in the church does not justify a withdrawal from God's project. Rather, it is important to remember that God does not call the perfect but the sinner to be converted and to contribute to God's kingdom. The experience of the resurrected crucified Christ has freed us from the pressures of judging the 'success' of our own or other people's contribution to God's creation. Rather, our experience of Jesus as the Christ is the foundation of our hope in God's ultimate fulfilment of his creative project in spite of the limitations and failures of our personal and communitarian responses. Nevertheless, such a hope needs our active participation, otherwise it is only a pious projection.

5.8 Conclusion

In this chapter we have discussed the relationship between God's call and the organisation of our communal response to this call. In the final chapter of this book we must return now to our efforts to understand God's call better. That means we must look at ways of letting ourselves be drawn more deeply into the mystery of God's creative and redemptive presence in our world.

6

GOD AND CHRISTIAN LIFE

6.0 Introduction

In this chapter I wish to discuss the resources available to individual Christians and to Christian communities who attempt both to deepen their understanding of God's call and to strengthen their response to this call in our world. I shall concentrate especially on the development of our relationship with God. What awareness do we have of God? What, if anything, do we expect from God? How can we develop our relationship with God?

In the first chapter of this book the question was raised how we can advance God's kingdom in this world. There we considered the way in which Jesus of Nazareth announced the closeness of God's kingdom and how he explained God's invitation to every human being to enter into a direct relationship with God. Thus, it became clear that no mediation of a third party, such as priests, temple cult or law, was necessary any longer for women, men and children who wish to turn to God. Rather every human being is called to rediscover their relationship with this loving God who is likened by Jesus to a loving parent and a friend. However, if our religious institutions can help humans to deepen this kind of immediate relationship with God, then their service ought to be welcomed; if they do not, then we are free to develop and grow beyond them.

This message about the possibility of a new, direct and close relationship with God is at the centre of Jesus's ministry. And as we have seen already in Chapter 1, the radical equality of all disciples, their readiness to respond to God, and their willingness to be surprised by God in this new relationship are the primary hallmarks of the emerging reign of God. In this chapter, then, we ought to consider this direct relationship with God more closely.

6.1 Developing our relationship with God

It is a sad fact that many Christians today feel unequipped with the bare spiritual necessities for developing their relationship with God. All too often their image of God is still that of a tyrannical father demanding the death of his son, or that of a supreme court judge who prepares for the ultimate inspection of our heavenly credentials after our death. It seems that in the Christian communities we are failing very often to encourage each other to grow in our relationship with God. Our contact with God is quite often still formal, distant, stale, heavily dependent on the proper mediation of our priests and pastors. We tend to leave the exploration of this contact with God to the specialists, the ordained clergy, the theologians, and the members of religious orders. Thus we fail to recognise that God has called each one of us into this new and immediate relationship with him. As Jesus emphasised again and again, God does not recognise special religious 'lobby groups', nor has he called for religious experts who would be more experienced in dealing with him than normal mortals.

In the early church the martyrs and saints were seen as such expert Christians who, as a result of their eternal proximity to God, could act as 'patrons' on behalf of their particular constituencies. They could put a good word in for us with the otherwise distant 'boss'. Hence, an image of a celestial civil-service machinery emerged which has been seen to be working vicariously on our behalf.[1]

Already in the gospels we are told of the failure of Jesus's closest followers and friends to understand God's call. Peter, for instance, is portrayed at times as a rather sad figure who missed the point again and again about the true requirements of responding to God's call. Peter is interested in a special deal, he longs for a special place in God's kingdom and thus does not grasp the egalitarian nature of God's emerging kingdom.

The inability or unwillingness of people to accept the fact that in Jesus Christ we have learnt once more that God wants to relate directly with each one of us and with all of us together is as old as the Christian movement itself. The gospels report at one and the same time the story of God's self-revelation in Jesus Christ and the story of human failure to come to terms with God's generous invitation to all of us to participate in the building of his kingdom.

Throughout the history of Christianity a two-tier system of discipleship has prevailed. Priests and members of religious orders have often been considered to be better disciples of Christ than ordinary lay folk. Whereas ordinary Christians were expected to follow Christ's precepts, the religious followed also Christ's three evangelical counsels, i.e. poverty, chastity and obedience. Later on, the secular clergy adopted chastity as their special mark of Christian service and discipleship. Hence a two-tier system of religious vocation has arisen according to which all are called to follow Christ, but some are called to follow Christ in a special way.

While there can, of course, be no doubt that each one of us has special gifts, special skills, a particular history and context to bring to the service of the Christian community, the classification of Christians into two divisions or ranks clearly contradicts God's universal call in Christ. As we have seen already, our spiritual authority rests in our response to God's call in whatever circumstances we may find ourselves. No Christian can therefore claim to be a more authentic or more genuine or more authoritative follower of Christ solely by referring to his or her status within the church. The final judgment on the authenticity of our response to God's call remains God's prerogative. In the meantime all expressions of our discipleship ought to be more radical, more perfect. God has not called us into half-hearted relationships. Rather, through Jesus we have learnt that God wishes to relate to all of me, and not only to certain dimensions of my personality at certain prescribed times during the week. Like the rich young man we may be depressed when we hear that God's call on us claims all aspects of our person and all aspects of our relational capacity, everything we are and have (Mt. 19:16–30).

To reach this total openness to God, to prepare myself for the bliss of the ultimate union between me and God requires a lifelong and often painful personal growth. As all of the great Christian mystics have emphasised, becoming aware of and accepting the desire to know God mark the beginning of a personal love relationship with God. Do we want to know God? Do we want to begin a never ending love affair with God? Do we want to risk our established emotional securities and possibly even our religious support structures while exploring this new and unknown intimacy with God? Do we want to be drawn further into the mystery of God? Are we prepared to suffer the pain of radical detachment which this journey unavoidably brings with it?

Detachment means to free ourselves from our clinging to goods and well-established securities, from everything which claims our total attention. But detachment does definitively not mean to gain a distance from involvement in God's creative project in this world. Are we prepared to sacrifice all of our preconceived images of God and of our own selves in this process of entering the mystery of God's presence in our lives? God's love for us is total; how total is our love for God?

All too frequently we misunderstand the meaning of love. We often speak of our love for people or things in order to underline how much we appreciate what we know about all of these. 'I love my home' then means that I am so fond of my home because I have got to know it and am so used to its comforts. Unfortunately, we may at times even relate to our spouses, children, friends, parents, brothers and sisters in this sense of 'love'. But love can mean something much more exciting and challenging. It can refer to my willingness to find out more about the other and hence ultimately also about myself. Love in this sense includes the attraction of the other as other. It includes the risks attached to any journey of discovery. It is aware of the threat which the disclosure of the unknown other as other may represent to me, especially when I have entered into an intimate relationship with this attractive other and thus have become very vulnerable myself.

Loving God is the most risky adventure. Opening myself to this radically other, to the one whom I can relate to only inadequately given the limitedness of my human nature makes great demands on me. Loving God is a journey into the unknown. However, we have been given God's Spirit as a guide on this journey. Thus, we are not alone on this adventurous journey of discovery. God's Spirit has become recognisable to us through Jesus Christ's ministry, death and resurrection. As this Spirit has strengthened Jesus in his radical understanding of God's call and his total response to this call, so it is here for our support. Most of all, it makes us aware that it is God's prior love for us that has enabled us in the first place to develop our love for him.

The 'prodigal father' waits for us until we return to him, and he opens his arms without dismay at the state in which we find ourselves when we return to him (Lk. 15:11–32). God respects us, he accepts our otherness, he does not want a standardised mass of identical daughters and sons. Rather, God invites us individually to develop and grow in our love relationship with him, each other, and his creation. In that sense, following Jesus does not mean to become his clone. It means to embark, in analogy to him, on our own freely chosen personal journey of deepening our relationship with God here in this world. However, following Jesus also means that, as he did, we have to pick up *our* cross and carry it (cf. Mk 8:34). The painfulness of detaching ourselves in order to pursue the love of God cannot be taken from us, nor the pain of discovering how much other God really is. Nor can we expect that our love relationship with God makes instant sense to anybody else. No love relationship can ever be fully understood by people who are not involved in it themselves.

Here we have reached a problem that every Christian community has to wrestle with. It must support the growth of the individual Christian's relationship with

God, it must respect this relationship, it must come to terms with the otherness of every individual relationship with God. Or expressed more positively, the Christian community is the only place where the individual Christian can expect to find support, critique and encouragement of his or her personal journey with God, precisely because all Christians have been called individually by God and received this call through the presence of God's Spirit in the community of Christ's disciples. If the Christian community wants to be faithful to this presence of the Spirit in it, it must honour and support the individual journey of each of its members. Instead of trying to subject every individual response to God to a particular norm of Christian 'behaviour', the Christian community ought to trust in the uniting force of this Spirit. Efforts to standardise or harmonise artificially the faith development of individual Christians cannot succeed. Rather, ultimate harmony among Christians can only be brought about by God who calls each Christian to embark on her or his individual journey with him. All members of the church must therefore learn how to cope with this otherness of each single fellow Christian and, even more challenging, how to relate to God's radical otherness.

Again, the presence of God's Spirit should guide us and comfort us when otherness becomes painful. It is this Spirit's characteristic to create unity among us. Christian unity in this sense remains ultimately a gift, it will always be the work of the Holy Spirit. But this gift must also be accepted by the individual members of the Christian community; that is to say, each member must help to build this communal unity. As we can rightly expect that we find support in the Christian community for our personal journeys in response to God's call, the church must be able to expect from each one of us the same kind of support for its communal response to God's call. The kingdom of God can only be advanced by all of us together.

How can we develop our personal and communal love relationship with this radically other God?

6.2 Christian prayer, worship and action

Prayer is the means by which we communicate with God, but also one of the ways by which God communicates with us. It is the primary way of encountering God's presence and his call. Although I cannot offer a comprehensive discussion of prayer in this book, I would like to draw the reader's attention to a few significant features of Christian prayer.

We have learnt from Jesus to address God as 'abba' (daddy). That means we are invited to relate to God in the closest possible form of human address. This address is in itself a sign of the intimacy of the relationship to which we are called. While God is referred to as father also in the Old Testament, he is never prayed to under this address. Jesus, however, prays to God only by addressing him as father. It has been rightly remarked that it is the arrival of children which makes somebody a father. In order to be a father one has to have children or at least one has to have had children.[2] Hence, in order to become our father, God is dependent on our readiness to become his daughters and sons. The intimate relationship between God and us depends on both partners. We can deprive God of some of his fatherhood by refusing to enter into the kind of intimate relationship which is characteristic of his creative plan for us.

Again, the point of this reflection on God as father is not the maleness of God. God is neither male nor female. Rather the point is to grasp the intimacy open to us when relating to God as person or persons.

The relational nature of God has found many expressions in the Christian tradition. The symbol of God's fatherhood has been extended into the threefold relationality of God as a Trinity of persons: Father, Son and Holy Spirit. The loving nature of God is wonderfully expressed in our classical trinitarian statements. Unfortunately however, we have all too often concentrated more on the arithmetic of trinitarian language, i.e. three in one, than on the expression of divine love relationship which is at the heart of our trinitarian discourse.[3]

In our prayer we can redress this imbalance and rediscover for ourselves the relational nature of God. By acknowledging God's 'fatherly' or 'motherly' readiness to reveal himself or herself to us we prepare ourselves for our exploration into God's mystery. By listening to God in silent meditation on his word in the Scriptures we allow God to speak to us and draw us along in the process of discovery of his closeness, but also of his radical otherness. By listening to his word in the Scriptures, by becoming aware of God's creative presence in our universe, and by praying to him together with others we allow God to address us also through his other children and thus to show us the variety of his relational activities. Moreover, the prayer of the church unites all Christians in their individual search for God's presence and recognises God's universal love and relational will.

There can be no deepening of any kind of relationship without communication. Hence, there can be no spiritual growth in Christian life without prayer. Though prayer is the necessary and most direct link between us and God, it is not the only connection.

Christian worship is a much extended prayer. It involves many more forms of expression than the direct prayer between individual Christians or groups of Christians and God usually does. Worship always includes prayer, but adds the physical orientation of men, women and children towards God. Silence, music, dance, and movement in general help us to explore also our emotional and physical dimensions as people before God. In Christian worship we aim at exploring a new and organic integration of our entire life in response to God's call.

Thus, in Christian worship we commit our entire created existence and our relationship to God's nature anew to God. In worshipping God we redirect the attention of all of our relational capacities to God: our relationship to each other in the local Christian community, our commitment to all human beings inside and outside the church, our relation to nature and the environment. And our dependence on God, on the other, and on the universe for our own growth are recognised, reflected and transformed in Christian worship. Especially, the celebration of the Eucharist (which we have treated already in Chapter 4) is a prime example of this rededication of our entire network of relationships to God. Pilgrimages are another apt example of our exploration of the rich rhythm of moving with God through his world.

Although Christian worship is an activity undertaken by groups of Christians together, not all Christian actions are worship in this direct meaning. There are also other forms of Christian action.

Some people would argue that the supreme Christian action is neither prayer nor worship, but active involvement on behalf of the poor and oppressed. I find it strange that the expressions of whole relationships which characterise the arrival of God's kingdom should be limited only to our attention to the poor. Of course, there can be no doubt that the very existence of poverty, illiteracy and oppression in our world is a terrible sign of the unredeemed and unwhole state of our life and a direct call on us Christians to become actively involved and show our human solidarity with the victims of injustice, poverty and oppression. However, the necessary attention to our poor and oppressed fellow humans need not diminish our equally necessary attention to our relationship with God and with ourselves. Rather, the wholeness which God wishes to give us calls us to a transformation of the entire network of relationships in which we live and can grow. As we have seen already above (2.5.5), love of God and love of neighbour are closely related, but not identical. Let me reflect upon this fact with regard to the value of Christian action.

6.3 Action and contemplation

There is really no necessary opposition between the mystical exploration of union with God and the active solidarity with the poor and oppressed. The great Spanish mystic John of the Cross (1515–61) is a good example in this respect. His efforts to know more about God always directed him back to the poor and needy, while his lifelong commitment to the poor and sick never reduced his enthusiasm for a closer relationship with God. In his ministry John appropriated Jesus's example in his own sixteenth-century Castillian context. It was in fact the image of the crucified Jesus that inspired John most of all to remain faithful in his own passionate and often painful search for God's presence.

John's traumatic experience of being totally rejected and castigated by his own fellow monks during his lengthy imprisonment within the Carmelite monastery at Toledo and his shattering experience of God's absence prepared him for a new and much deeper discovery of God's presence, but also of God's otherness.[4] In this dark night of the soul John understood that it is otherness which makes the love of God possible in the first instance. The experience of God's absence had thus become the foundational experience of the real presence of God.[5] And yet again, this new discovery of God's otherness directed John to work even more committedly in his ministry to the materially and spiritually poor. Contemplation and action form a unity in John's understanding of Christian faith.

There is also another dimension to John's terrible experiences at his monastic imprisonment which we ought to examine here. John's imprisonment and torture at the hand of his fellow monks also document the pain which our closest church community can at times impose on us. John's deep personal experience of God's call was perceived as a threat by many of his fellow monks. As Jesus had been rejected by the most serious observers of religion in his time, so was John rejected by some of the most seriously committed members of his religious order.

Why is it that we are so likely to reject those whose spiritual energy and active solidarity stem from their love relationship with God? Do these Christian figures make us insecure because they threaten the normality of our religious attitudes? Do the radical lifestyle and praxis of John of the Cross and of Jesus manifest such a restless search for God's own will that we have to fear that our own haphazard ways of following Jesus are exposed? It seems that we either elevate people such as Jesus and John to the distance of the pedestal of sainthood (preferably after their death) or we reject them as religious trouble makers (usually during their ministry). One lesson to be learnt from this is that following Christ is a dangerous business. At times we may become very lonely in the midst of the community of which we are a part. Responding to God in a radical way may then prove a dangerous religious course of action. However, precisely in this traumatic experience of the cross, of rejection by our very own Christian community, we have nothing other to rely upon than the direct relationship with God, although we have, of course, been developing this relationship within the community of Christians.

Moreover, as John's story underlines so forcefully, God wants to be loved for his own sake and not for the sake of finding a ready comfort for our tears. The experience of the dark night of my soul exposes both my uncritical reliance on a communal stability and my uncritical reliance on images of God, both communal and personal, which do not allow God to be known for what he truly is. The dark night of the soul is first and foremost then an experience of the true conditions of love. I must attend to God, the other, as other without conditions; I must attend to God for God's sake.

If Christian contemplation is an exercise in discovering the otherness of God so that we can truly love him, it is at the same time a most fitting preparation for the discovery of the other whom I want to serve for his or her own sake. Contemplation offers an opportunity for discovering my genuine calling and the true needs of the other – including the other within myself. Hence Christian contemplation is a necessary dimension of authentic Christian faith-praxis. It directs me to the needs of the other and it protects the other from an imposition of my own needs on him or her.

There can be no doubt whatsoever that God has called us to contribute to his creative project by acting in this world. But there can be equally no doubt that any action on behalf of God's project requires to be tested in terms of whose spirit operates in it. Do I help the poor because they need my help or do I seek a justification for my existence? Do I understand the true needs of the materially and spiritually poor in this world or do I project my own insecurities on them? Do I try to love the people I wish to help, that is to say, do I try to discover their otherness and to respect their dignity as equal partners in God's kingdom? Do I allow myself to grow in relationship with God while being engaged in helping my neighbour and while attending to the needs of our battered eco-system?

Contemplation, it seems, is the necessary way of developing our fourfold relationship with God, with each other, with the universe and with our own often hidden self. Contemplation is then not an optional extra for Christians but an essential part of our response to God's call. Karl Rahner's famous dictum that 'the devout Christian of the future will either be a "mystic", one who has "experienced" something, or he will cease to be anything at all' sums up this section very concisely.[6]

6.4 Resources of Christian faith

God wants our free response to his call. Therefore we must be actively engaged in helping to establish such structures in our Christian communities which facilitate this free response. Only when we are engaged in striving to become credible witnesses to this God-given freedom within our own communities, can we hope to be taken seriously in our emancipatory concerns by the world at large. Unfortunately, we Christians have often failed to acknowledge the liberational and emancipatory potential of the gospel. Instead we have devised schemes of containing spiritual freedom and of subordinating our personal growth before God to the demands of conformist church structures or of the versatile pressures from our socio-political and cultural contexts. Often our concerns for the future stability of the church have outweighed our attention to the coming kingdom of God. We have on the whole much lacked the necessary eschatological drive, and preferred to organise our ultimate home in the here and now, in the given co-ordinates of church and society. Thus, we have responded more to our own unreflected needs, rather than concentrating on the requirements of responding to God's call in Christ. How can we break out from this self-imposed imprisonment? What resources are available to us for our spiritual renewal?

6.4.1 READING THE SCRIPTURES

Reading the biblical texts offers us the primary – though as we are going to see, not the only – opportunity of reconsidering the possibilities of divine–human relationship.

Unfortunately, the biblical texts have often been

subjected to strange practices of exploitation. In some churches they have been used more as proof-texts for ecclesiastical decisions, while in other churches they have been elevated to a sacred status far beyond the reach of any necessary critique or questioning. Moreover, theologians in general and biblical scholars in particular have made us insecure by questioning both the historical veracity of stories and events reported by and reflected upon in biblical texts and the general reliability of their truth claims. This situation does not seem to recommend the biblical texts as guides in our efforts at reconsidering God's relationship to us and our relationship with God.

This chapter is not the place for a detailed consideration of the nature and rules of biblical interpretation.[7] Rather, here I wish to emphasise the spiritual potential of the biblical texts.

One does not need to be a professional theologian or biblical exegete in order to read the biblical texts. The Bible speaks about God, about his call on humanity, and about humanity's response or non-response to that call. The Scriptures invite every reader to follow their concerns, i.e. the story and contemplation of God's presence in our universe. Of course, each text of the Hebrew Scriptures, i.e. what we Christians call the Old Testament, and every text within the New Testament tells us a story about God's relationship with his people, though from the distinct perspective of certain persons or communities of believers. Thus, the very existence of the Bible is a witness to people's diverse responses to God's call in specific periods of human history. Therefore, it is crucial to respect the biblical texts as human texts, written by humans for humans, written from a limited cultural perspective and read within the particular horizon of people. Hence, the biblical texts stand firmly within the Jewish and Christian traditions of responding to God's call in human history. Every effort to isolate these texts from these concrete traditions will miss their true spiritual potential.

David Tracy has therefore correctly challenged the old Catholic view that 'Scripture and tradition' together form the norms of Christian faith, but also the old Protestant view that 'Scripture alone' offers a reliable guide for the believer. Instead he proposes that we always see 'Scripture within tradition', because every biblical text points to its own context out of which it originally emerged.[8]

The biblical texts are witnesses from within our traditions of responding to God's call in Israel and in Jesus Christ. For the reader they function as bridges between God's previous self-manifestations and his presence today. They invite us to understand God's creative project within the history of the people whom he called to participate in it. And they invite us to explore how we today can understand God's mysterious presence and respond best to his ongoing project. But the biblical texts offer even more than this primary invitation to relate and respond to God.

The Scriptures also challenge us to tackle our lack of response, they help us to rediscover ways of returning to God, and they provide us with a language through which we can relate to God. In this sense they are inexhaustible. They offer the Christian believer and the Christian community at the same time information, inspiration, examples, paradigms, challenge, companionship, admonition, comfort, and spiritual instruction. They are then the primary resource of all Christian renewal. Yet they are not the only resource.

6.4.2 EXPLORING THE CHRISTIAN TRADITION

The history of the Christian movement, what we often call 'the Christian tradition', is another vital resource for efforts of Christian self-reflection and spiritual reorientation. 'The Christian tradition' is in reality a collective name for all the many local traditions of Christian responses to God's call in Christ throughout the last twenty centuries. We have already seen that tradition is an ambiguous phenomenon and that we cannot just adopt any previous generation's way of responding to God's call as a sure model for us today (cf. above 4.2). Rather we ought to learn from our explorations in Christian history about more and less appropriate communal and individual efforts at responding to God's call in Christ.

For some people the Christian tradition consists first and foremost in its accumulation of official church doctrines. For others the Christian tradition refers to the uninterrupted series of theological restatements of the Christian faith. For yet another group of people the Christian tradition means the continuation of Christian worship. And there are many more ways of referring to this great and diverse movement of Christian responses to God's call. As the ecumenical movement during this century has established by means of painful experience and growth, the unity of the Christian tradition lies hidden not just in the doctrinal, theological and liturgical dimensions of Christian faith. Rather Christian unity is unity in the Spirit that welcomes originality, diversity and openness in response to God's call.

This new appreciation of the spiritual unity of all Christian disciples facilitates the development of more authentic local reponses to God's call today. But it also sharpens our view for authentic responses in our past.

Once we have freed ourselves from the constraints of uniformity we may become more sensitive towards the particularities of *other* Christian responses past and present. Suddenly then, our Christian tradition becomes a rich resource for us on our journey towards a better faith-praxis in a more authentic faith community.

Not just the prophets, the mystics, the saints, the founders and members of religious orders, the church leaders and the well-known and well-documented lives of certain Christians gain a new interest for us, but the story of every individual Christian response and every communal effort of transforming this world in response to God's invitation may become a rich resource for us today. Church history suddenly takes on spiritual dimensions. It cannot therefore be left any longer to the exclusive attention of antiquaries and scholarly experts.

We must promote the development of a Christian solidarity with all the Christians and Christian communities of the past together with whom we are building the great Christian tradition. The study of this tradition in all its local manifestations becomes a life-giving task for us all. But this study needs a critical self-awareness and an ongoing discussion of criteria of Christian authenticity. This need for critical and self-critical reflection brings us to Christian theology as yet another rich resource for Christian renewal.

6.4.3 THE NEED FOR CHRISTIAN THEOLOGY

Theology is necessary for us as a means of gaining critical distance from our own faith-practice. How would we ever know what we are doing when we are exploring our relationship with God, if we never had the opportunity to ask questions, to consider alternative ways of responding to God's call, and to reflect upon what may count as authentic Christian response to God? But theology does not only help us to develop ways of understanding our tradition and our present attempts at exploring God's presence in this world. Rather it helps us also to refine our language in which we talk about God's mysterious presence in Israel, in Jesus Christ, in the church and in our lives and communities today. Theology provides us with theories of better Christian praxis. Yet it also keeps us in touch with the search for meaning in other realms of life (literature, art, music etc.) and in other cultures. Theology helps us to correlate our explorations in Christian faith with the ongoing efforts at understanding our world and its ultimate meaning. Theology then is one of the many necessary services (or ministries) in the church.

Not everybody experiences the need to become a professional theologian himself or herself. But everybody in the church is affected by theology and therefore must have an interest, in that it is well done and that it communicates its reflections properly on all levels of the church. Because only if the fruits of theological reflection are available to the community at large can theology function as a spiritual resource for the church. However, if theological reflection cannot unfold its constructive and critical task because it is elitist or because it is hindered by sections of the church itself, then the entire community runs the risk of missing the challenges of one important resource for its continuous spiritual renewal.[9]

Naturally, there is no guarantee that all theologians will fulfil the tasks with which they have been charged by their respective communities and their societies. Theological self-critique must be part of the task. But without theology, that means without the continuous and critical reminder of old and new ways of understanding God's call and of responding to it, the entire community is in danger of losing its way, runs the risk of missing important aspects for its consideration of what it means to develop adequate discipleship today. Theology is no luxury for the Christian church, rather it is a hard and often frustrating work on behalf of the Christian community which therefore deserves the strong and critical support of the entire community.

6.5 The end of the journey

We have reached the final section of this book. Much has been said about God and about our feeble efforts at responding to his majestic invitation to help in the building of his kingdom. Much more could be said, and, I am painfully aware, much more would need to be said about the excitement which God's call has brought to our community. But maybe at least a beginning has been made by concentrating anew on God's creative project and on our involvement in it. To be sure, our individual contribution to this universal project is very limited indeed. But our participation in the whole project counts. We have not been asked by God to run his project for him; rather we have been invited to contribute to it in whatever way we can. And we have been asked to contribute to it in such a way that we build up God's own community, a community that is ready to transform this world and to be transformed by God at the same time.

The end of the journey is not known to us. God will surprise us at the end. But this hope in God's surprising action has led to many powerful, though necessarily limited, symbolic expressions. Shalom, eternal life, the kingdom of God, paradise, peace, and harmony figure prominently among those linguistic efforts of talking about that which by virtue of our human limitedness we can never fully grasp. Moreover, we have learnt from mystical thinkers, such as Hildegard of Bingen, Julian of Norwich, Teresa of Avila and John of the Cross, that no language, no concept, no symbol can ever express the greatness of God's love for his creation. We must therefore face the paradox of speaking about our ultimate expectations, but at the same time allow that they too will be purified by the fire of the burning bush. As individuals we are invited to follow the example of Christ, to accept our call and our cross and follow him to eternal glory. As a community of Christian disciples we have been called to gather in order to provide space for the presence and the power of the living Christ in this world. Are we ready to accept this twofold call and be transformed by Christ's presence? Are we willing to become agents of God's creative project? Are we prepared to embark on this communal journey of discovering more about God, more about his otherness and his creative project, more about our ultimate end in life?

NOTES

Chapter 1: Advancing the Kingdom of God (pp 1–23)

1 Gabriel Daly, 'Catholicism and Modernity', *Journal of the American Academy of Religion* 53 (1985), 773.
2 Cf. ibid., 781ff.
3 Cf. Jean-François Lyotard. *The Postmodern Condition: A Report on Knowledge*, trans. Geoff Bennington and Brian Massumi (Manchester: Manchester University Press, 1986).
4 See Charles Taylor, *Sources of the Self: The Making of Modern Identity* (Cambridge, Mass.: Harvard University Press, 1989); and Paul Ricœur, *Oneself as Another*, trans. Katleen Blamey (Chicago: University of Chicago Press, 1992).
5 Patrick Kavanagh, *The Complete Poems*. Ed. Peter Kavanagh (Newbridge: Goldsmith Press, 1987). See, for example, the poems 'God in Woman' (237) and 'Canal Bank Walk' (294f.).
6 Gotthold Hasenhüttl, *Herrschaftsfreie Kirche: Sozio-theologische Grundlegung* (Düsseldorf: Patmos, 1974).

Chapter 2: Building the Faith Community (pp 24–4)

1 See Anne Carr, 'The God Who Is Involved', *Theology Today* 38 (1981), 314–28.
2 Cf. Paul M. Zulehner, 'Gemeinde', in Peter Eicher, ed., *Neues Handbuch theologischer Grundbegriffe*, vol. 2 (München: Kösel, 1984), 52–65.

Chapter 3: Death and Life in Jesus Christ (pp 45–65)

1 Gabriel Daly, *Creation and Redemption* (Dublin: Gill and Macmillan, 1988), 204.
2 Ibid., 205.
3 Cf. Eberhard Jüngel, *Tod*. 3rd ed. (Stuttgart: Kreuz Verlag, 1973), 21.
4 Quoted in Hans Küng, *Eternal Life?* Trans. Edward Quinn (London: Collins, 1984), 52.
5 *Ganztodtheorie* in German.
6 Jüngel, *Tod*, op. cit. 171.
7 Ibid., 152.
8 Ibid., 171.
9 *Catechism of the Catholic Church* (Dublin: Veritas, 1994).
10 The reference within this quotation is to the Constitution *Gaudium of Spes* of the Second Vatican Council.
11 Karl Rahner, 'Tod', in Karl Rahner, ed., *Herders Theologisches Taschenlexikon*, vol. 7 (Freiburg, Basel, Vienna: Herder, 1973), 279–84, here 280 (my translation).

12 Ibid., 279 (my translation).
13 See Jüngel, *Tod*, op. cit., 42.
14 See Martin Heidegger, *Sein und Zeit*, 13th ed. (Tübingen: Niemeyer, 1976), 235–67.

Chapter 4: Eucharistic Discipleship (pp 66–89)

1 For a discussion of criteria of interpreting this tradition see Werner G. Jeanrond, *Theological Hermeneutics: Development and Significance* (London: SCM, 1994), 159–82 (chapter 7).
2 Dietrich Bonhoeffer, *Nachfolge*, 13th ed. (München: Kaiser, 1982), 62 (my translation).
3 Ibid., 64 (my translation).
4 Cf. Johann Baptist Metz, *Faith in History and Society: Toward a Practical Fundamental Theology*, trans. David Smith (New York: Seabury-Crossroad, 1980).
5 For an excellent discussion of the history and the significance of the Eucharist see David Power, *The Eucharistic Mystery: Revitalizing the Tradition* (New York: Crossroad, and Dublin: Gill and Macmillan, 1992)
6 Metz, *Faith in History and Society*, op. cit., 90.
7 See Wolfhart Pannenberg, *Christian Spirituality and Sacramental Community* (London: Darton, Longman and Todd, 1983), 47: 'The Eucharist manifests the mystery of the church, the communion of believers united by the communion of each with Christ, and symbolizes the eschatological unity of all humanity.'
8 For more information see David Power, *The Eucharistic Mystery*, op. cit.
9 A reminder that the point here is not to declare God to be 'male'. The male form of discourse is used in order not to complicate the presentation of my thoughts. For a more balanced approach to discourse on God see Elizabeth A. Johnson, *She Who Is: The Mystery of God in Feminist Theological Discourse* (New York: Crossroad, 1993).

Chapter 5: Eucharistic Discipleship (pp 90–112)

1 Robert L. Peabody, 'Authority', in *International Encyclopedia of the Social Sciences* I (Collier and Macmillan, 1968), 473–77, here 473.
2 See Gerd Theissen, *Soziologie der Jesusbewegung: Ein Beitrag zur Entstehungsgeschichte des Urchristentums*. Theologische Existenz heute 194, 3rd ed. (Munich: Kaiser, 1981), 14ff.
3 See Norbert Brox, *Kirchengeschichte des Altertums*, 2nd ed. (Düsseldorf: Patmos, 1986), 90ff.
4 See my critique of the two-class system in the Roman Catholic Church in 'One Church: Two Classes? The Lesson of History', in Seán MacRéamoinn, ed., *Pobal: the laity in Ireland* (Dublin: Columba Press, 1986), 22–34.

5 *Lumen Gentium* 7.

6 Einar Sigurbjörnsson, *Ministry within the People of God: The Development of the Doctrines on the Church and on the Ministry in the Second Vatican Council's De Ecclesia*. Studia Theologica Lundensia 34 (Lund: Gleerup, 1974), 84.

7 See Gabriel Daly, 'Catholicism and Modernity', *Journal of the American Academy of Religion* 53 (1985), 773–96.

8 Leonardo Boff, *Church: Charism and Power: Liberation Theology and the Institutional Church*, trans. John W. Dierckmeier (London: SCM, 1985), 48.

9 Ibid., 55f.

10 For a detailed discussion of the problems and opportunities involved in this process of interpretation see Werner G. Jeanrond, *Theological Hermeneutics: Development and Significance* (London: SCM, 1994).

11 See Edward Schillebeeckx, *The Church with a Human Face: A New and Expanded Theology of Ministry*, trans. John Bowden (London: SCM, 1985), 156ff.

12 See A. T. & R. P. C. Hanson, *The Identity of the Church: A Guide to Recognising the Contemporary Church* (London: SCM, 1987), 144.

13 See Karl Rahner, 'Autorität', in *Christlicher Glaube in moderner Gesellschaft*, vol. 14 (Freiburg i.B., Basel, Vienna: Herder, 1982), 8f.

14 See Richard Niebuhr, *Christ and Culture* (New York: Harper & Row, 1951).

15 Robert J. Schreiter, *Constructing Local Theologies* (London: SCM, 1985), 93.

16 Cf. ibid., 94

17 See Jürgen Moltmann, *The Church in the Power of the Spirit: A Contribution to Messianic Ecclesiology*, trans. Margaret Kohl (London: SCM, 1977), 248ff.

18 In this context one may wish to consider, for instance, the need to assess Christian contributions to the new efforts of uniting Europe. See, for example, Werner G. Jeanrond, 'The Christian Voice in an Integrated Europe', *Doctrine and Life* 40 (1990), 340–7.

19 Johann Baptist Metz has repeatedly stressed this point. See his *Zur Theologie der Welt* (Mainz: Grünewald, and München: Kaiser, 1968), and his *Faith in History and Society: Towards a Practical Fundamental Theology*, trans. David Smith (New York: Seabury-Crossroad, 1980).

Chapter 6: Eucharistic Discipleship (pp 113–134)

1 See Peter Brown, *The Cult of the Saints: Its Rise and Function in Latin Christianity* (Chicago: University of Chicago Press, 1981).

2 See Janet Martin Soskice, 'The Christian Rhetoric of God and Human Relational Experience', in James M. Byrne, ed., *The Christian Understanding of God Today* (Dublin: Columba Press, 1993), 112–18.

3 See Werner G. Jeanrond, 'The Question of God Today', in *The Christian Understanding of God Today*, op. cit., 9–23.

4 See Richard P. Hardy, *Search for Nothing: The Life of John of the Cross* (New York: Crossroad, 1987), 61–78.

5 See *John of the Cross, Selected Writings*, ed. Kieran Kavanaugh. The Classics of Western Spirituality (New York and Mahwah: Paulist Press, 1987), esp. 155–209.

6 Karl Rahner, *Theological Investigations*, vol. 7, trans. David Bourke (London: Darton, Longman & Todd, 1973), 15. Cf. also *Theological Investigations*, vol. 20, trans. Edward Quinn (London: Darton, Longman & Todd, 1981), 149.

7 See Werner G. Jeanrond, *Text and Interpretation as Categories of Theological Thinking*, trans. Thomas J. Wilson (Dublin: Gill and Macmillan, and New York: Crossroad, 1988); and *Theological Hermeneutics: Development and Significance* (London: SCM, 1994).

8 See David Tracy, 'On Reading the Scriptures Theologically', in Bruce D. Marshall, ed., *Theology and Dialogue: Essays in Conversation with George Lindbeck* (Notre Dame: Notre Dame University Press, 1990), 37f.

9 See Claude Geffré and Werner G. Jeanrond, eds., *Why Theology? Concilium* (London: SCM, and Maryknoll: Orbis, 1994:6).

INDEX

Family, 12, 68, 69, 92
Feminism, 5. *see also* Church: role
    of women
Forgiveness, 30, 78, 87

Geffré, Claude, 138
Geldof, Bob, 66, 73
God
    absence of God, 124–5
    creative project. *see* Creation
    God beyond God, 8
    God as Trinity. *see* Trinity
    image of God, 114, 117, 120–21
    kingdom of God. *see* Kingdom
    love of God. *see* Love
    reign of God. *see* Kingdom
    Spirit of God. *see* Spirit
Grace, 27, 29, 30, 64, 87

Hanson, Anthony, 137
Hanson, Richard, 137
Hardy, Richard, 138
Hasenhüttl, Gotthold, 135
Heaven, 36, 53, 114
Heidegger, Martin, 61–2
Hell, 36, 53
Hermeneutics. *see* Biblical
    Interpretation
Hierarchy, 16, 21, 57, 70, 71, 90,
    102
Hildegard of Bingen, 134
Holocaust, 5
Hope, 37, 45, 46, 61, 63, 64, 65, 66,
    67–8, 85, 87, 111, 133
Hosea, 47

Immortality, 47–54
Inculturation, 106, 108, 110. *see also*
    Culture
Intercommunion, 81–2
Isaiah, 47
Israel, 11, 14, 24, 28, 38, 42, 43, 68,
    75, 77, 129, 132

James, 100
Jesus Christ, ix, 1, 9, 11, 12–13, 14,
    18, 19, 23, 24, 25, 26, 37, 38,
    42, 43, 45–7, 50, 56–64,

    67–74, 75–89, 90, 95, 100,
    102, 106–9, 113–25, 132, 134
John (Gospel), 11, 13
John of the Cross, 123–5, 134, 138
Johnson, Elizabeth, 136
Julian of Norwich, 134
Jüngel, Eberhard, 54–5, 135, 136

Kavanagh, Patrick, 14, 135
Kingdom of God (Reign of God),
    ix, x, 1, 10–23, 24–5, 32, 33,
    35, 39, 43, 67, 68, 70, 74, 79,
    82, 85, 86, 87, 88, 111,
    113–14, 115, 120, 123, 127,
    133. *see also* Eternal Life

Laity, 8, 10, 21, 23, 24, 93, 94–6,
    100
Leadership, x, 25, 30, 76, 77, 79, 89,
    90–112
Liberation, 5, 28, 66, 127
Limbo, 36, 53
Liturgy, 76, 82–8, 107, 130. *see also*
    Worship
Loisy, Alfred, 67
Love, x, 12, 13, 14, 15, 23, 54, 64,
    68, 69, 72, 74, 77, 78, 80, 116,
    117, 118, 120, 121, 123, 124,
    125, 134
Luke (Gospel), 11, 118
Luther, Martin, 29–30
Lyotard, Jean-François, 135

MacRéamoinn, Seán, 136
Mark (Gospel), 11, 19, 71, 118, 120
Martin Soskice, Janet, 138
Martyr, 114
Materialism, 45, 59–60
Matthew (Gospel), 11, 42, 80, 116
Metz, Johann Baptist, 77, 136, 137
Ministries (in the Church), 8–9, 10,
    15–19, 89, 90, 100–103, 107,
    114, 123, 125
Modernity, 2, 3–10, 96
Moltmann, Jürgen, 137
Monastic Movement, 94, 124. *see*
    also Religious Orders
Moses, 14, 28, 43

DATE DUE

#47-0108 Peel Off Pressure Sensitive